Enjoy What We Have

Enjoy What We Have,

A Commitment of Love

A memoir

by

Philip J. Palladino

Enjoy What We Have, A Commitment of Love

Copyright © 2019 by Philip J. Palladino

Cover design by Philip J. Palladino
Book design by Philip J.Palladino

Printed in the United States of America
The Troy Book Makers • Troy, New York • thetroybookmakers.com

To order additional copies of this memoir,
contact your favorite local bookstore
or visit www.shoptbmbooks.com
or Amazon.com

ISBN: 978-1-61468-509-8

Cover: In the Samnite ruins in Pietrabbondante, Italy. The pillars and the arch date from the Second Century B.C.E. The strong pillars crafted from polygonal stones support this arch that has a keystone in the center. Despite centuries of storms, warfare and neglect, the pillars are strong, the arch remains.

To my late wife Phyllis who made even the tough times enjoyable, and to our children, Dan and Meg.

1. Myrtle Beach

As the ocean sky darkens, the warmth of the spa protects us from the east wind. The waves crash closer, into our little oasis, but we're at peace. We lie impregnable in the hot tub.

Phyllis and I had grown tired of the winter of 2001. It was not an unusual winter, just as long and cold as almost any other, running from November 1 until April 30. We had been living in Austerlitz, New York since 1973. Our two children, Dan and Meg, in their late twenties, are natives of this hamlet which produces very few. When we retired from teaching in 1998, our combined careers exceeded sixty-five years, most of those years in Chatham High School. Phyllis and I look for an opportunity to escape for a couple of weeks in March. Myrtle Beach, South Carolina! Why not enjoy the weather there?

We drive all day to Charlottesville, Virginia, searching for spring. A scraping halt into a slight snow bank indicates that the winter spell has not been broken. A tinkle of ice says "gotcha" as I push open the driver's side door. The shell of winter has encapsulated the car. It spreads down the windshield. With a gloved hand, I balance on the ice tortoised car toward the passenger side where I break through the shell. Phyllis waits anxiously.

"Tell me, again, why we left Austerlitz?" Phyllis asks.

We shuffle to the Comfort Inn office and to our room with our one overnight bag. In the North, we would have simply turned up the heat. This frugal hotel had decided that heat is not needed after March 1. We are forced into each other's arms for warmth. Not a bad idea. I pity the single travelers.

By ten o'clock the next day, we're inside Monticello, Jefferson's cold mansion. We had been attracted here because it is an old presidential home, but also because our own house is said to be a Jeffersonian design. We find out that's true, but other than some exterior balance in our architecture, our house is a dwarf. We don't linger at Monticello. Winter is still howling at our backs as we head south.

A progressive spring unfolds. Budding wild cherry trees near Richmond and Petersburg. Tulips, daffodils and other staunch soldiers of spring are in full array along the rest areas and highways. Plenty of warmth thaws our bodies as Phyllis pulls into South of the Border travel complex, the South Carolina welcome mat. Breakfast, lunch, lodging, beachwear, souvenirs and fireworks. "Get them here!" We purchase two T-shirts emblazoned "Sparky's fireworks."

Over the final fifteen miles, we chant the label of each new wonder. "Palm trees!" "Magnolias!" "Green grass!" "Blue Herons!"

Our resort is an unattractive, solitary building, three stories high. Apparently facing the street. Little weeds stray out of planters of drifted sand in the parking lot. No welcome center. There must be good news in this, I think as we haul out our suitcases. The place is both elevator and valet free. The outdoor stairs to the third-floor deck, a virtual mountain.

I turn the key, push open the door. Wow! The ocean fills the room. Hushed, we tip-toe to the balcony opposite the door; a flock of pelicans squawk a hello chorus. The warm light brown sandy beach beneath the balcony forms a welcome arm. The ocean, 30 feet away. We uncork our Blackstone Merlot and collapse in the parlor of the pelicans and gulls. "Unbelievable!" Phyllis chortles.

Meg and Dan have decided to join us for this trip. The phone disrupts our ecstasy. It's Meg who describes her flight plan. I respond to her so Phyllis gets the gist of the conversation. "Sure, we'll be there at eleven on Monday morning. The airport is only a few miles away... We'll find you. It's very small...Wait till you see this place," I say. "And Dan's coming on Tuesday."

"He's missing out on some good beach time!" Phyllis says as she rises from the chair on the deck. "I'm going to rest before we hit the beach." The ecstatic moment has fleeted as Phyllis goes to lie down in the magnificent bedroom, bedecked in sea shells and photos of ocean fish.

Late Monday morning, Meg stands with her red backpack, waiting in front of the terminal at Myrtle Beach airport. Her tiny dark glasses and sun hat indicate her readiness for R and R. "Can we get some lunch?" Meg asks. "I only had time for a little breakfast."

Taco Bell is nearby with vegetarian food. Quick service. Cheap and familiar. As we walk into the little dining area, a strange thing happens. Phyllis suddenly seems dazed. "I'll have…a sunny…Taco Bell." She slumps into a chair.

Meg and I look quizzically at each other and at Phyllis, who gazes disinterestedly toward the window. I order a bean burrito and a glass of water for her. Over the years, whenever we ate at Taco Bell, she had ordered the same. She was a cheap date. "Are you okay?" I ask as I slide onto a stool next to her. Phyllis gives a detached nod.

"You'll feel better after you eat." Meg assures her when she delivers the trayful of burritos, tacos, and cups of water.

The cloud that had enveloped Phyllis lifts as the meal progresses. She returns to the conversation and to our world by the end of the meal. I ask her "What do you think happened?"

"I don't know," she replies. "I just feel very tired." We find our way back to our resort and walk the beach.

Dan joins us on Tuesday with fresh energy. The sun showers us from above and reflects from below as Phyllis and I walk arm in arm for miles on the warm sand. Dan tries the ocean water. The rest of us cool our feet in the lapping waves among the abundant starfish and shells. The gulls have their fill. Flocks of

9

pelicans ply the shallow waters while dolphins leap in the distance. Fisherman, surf boarders, wind-surfers, and kite flyers create a dazzling tapestry. A piper cub buzzes above with a banner streaming from its tail, *The Hard Rock Cafe.* When the sun sets behind us, we find the hot tub on the ground floor, adjacent to the beach. The four of us relax there with glasses of Cabernet. Revitalization in process, just like on TV.

Dan and Meg party with me on a couple of nights. Phyllis excuses herself, "I'm going to read, you have a good time."

"What's up with Mom?" Dan asks.

Meg says, "It's her vacation too. She can do what she wants."

"She needs her rest; it's been a long trip," I add in Phyllis's defense.

After a few days of sun, Meg returns to Boston. Dan joins us in the churning hot tub in the evening. Gushing spigots massage our lower backs and ribs. A storm brews off-shore. The edge of the storm clouds is sharp. It hovers near enough that we see the edge, but people play on the beach in the sun. Four-foot high waves pound the shore. Surfers love them. Daring wind-surfers try to catch an updraft. We cheer their triumphs as we rehash the week. The deepening storm, the menacing waves, the hissing sandy wind effects no harm. We only bail out when ocean waves swamp our little space.

After Dan's flight departs on early Friday morning, Phyllis and I have a final day to explore. Between raindrops and downpours, we make our way to Greenwood Gardens. Showy azaleas, sparkling fountains, sculpted terraces adorned with more sculpture make us want to extend our stay. Instead, we slog through the day, order pizza, finish the Cabernet, and sleep well.

The next morning, we head north. Phyllis drives when we reach the interstate. Every two hours we switch, and then, rest for the night in Williamsburg, Virginia. Eventually, we reach the Northeast where it's still winter. Glistening snow defines our pasty mud driveway. The roaring furnace welcomes us home.

2. The Brown Envelope

The refreshment of Myrtle Beach brings us home to face a personal challenge, far more difficult than the weather. As we shop for fresh spring clothes at the Berkshire Mall in Pittsfield, Massachusetts, Phyllis picks up a few items and then stops in a daze. It reminds me of Taco Bell, but she seems still in tune with herself. "I feel strange," she says softly, "I have to sit down." I usher her to the chairs near the fitting room where she remains resting for about fifteen minutes. Rather than hover too close creating additional anxiety, I keep an eye on her from a distance. When she recovers, Phyllis says "I just needed to rest. I need some energy."

"Let's go next door to the Coffee Roasters," I say while I rearrange the three bags of clothes into my left hand. Her hand is cold as I hold it during the short walk to the coffee bar. We share a raspberry scone, with our black coffees.

"What was that about?" I ask.

"I don't know." she replies, "Maybe leftover fatigue from the Myrtle Beach trip, I'm okay." We snack in silence. "Let's go home!" we say in unison.

A few days later, the sun heats up the porch. It feels good to sit in the early spring sun. I run to the kitchen to answer the phone, then pick up some bills to work on. Phyllis quietly comes in from the porch. Appearing slightly dazed, she says, "It happened again."

"What happened?" I ask.

"That strange feeling. I don't like it." She dials a number. "I'm calling Dr. Sparks."

The January checkup revealed nothing but good health and the promise of a long life. What could be wrong that wasn't revealed then? Phyllis gets an appointment for the next day when Dr. Sparks performs a quick neurological evaluation. Nothing amiss with balance, walking, talking, hearing, memory, coordination. Her tongue is normal. The nurse calls me into the exam room. Sparks states her concern. "Whatever is going on is from the heart or the brain. We need to do some tests."

Sparks sets up an MRI in Hudson to check the brain, and an appointment to have a twenty-four-hour heart monitor at Columbia Memorial Hospital. Sparks describes the MRI: "It's a scan that takes pictures of your brain. You slide into a tube. There will be a lot of noise. It doesn't hurt. It takes about forty-five minutes."

Phyllis is visibly agitated by the description, so Sparks prescribes Valium to relieve claustrophobia. "Take it fifteen minutes before the scan, and you'll be fine."

It's difficult for me to process this sudden turn of events, from perfect health to major tests to key parts of the body. Parts of which we only have one. Parts on which life depends. Nothing has happened. I practice calm and courage. Whatever is going on can't be so bad. We'll get through it. I'm certain the results of these tests will be negative for whatever they are supposed to discover.

A few days later in a Hudson, New York clinic, Phyllis pops a Valium while the technician waits.

My certainty evaporates as I see Phyllis strapped and wrapped into the MRI chamber. The technician makes her comfortable in the cold room. He places a cushion under her knees, a washcloth over her eyes, two blankets for warmth, and earplugs. In the waiting room, I hear the clanking and buzzing of the magnetic resonance imaging machine. The clanging is from another world, garbage cans early morning in the alley. The buzzing is like a jolt of electricity. All harmless, except to the ears. The cacophony ceases after about forty-five minutes. When the machine is silent, the technician makes a phone call.

He reports to us, "The doctor wants some pictures with contrast. A nurse will be here shortly to inject some dye to help the process."

Tension. Something is not going well. Contrast, what is that?

I deposit my wallet with credit cards and my car keys into a small locker, so they won't be drawn into the magnetic field. Credit cards and driver's license perish in that chamber. Optimism does, too. The room temperature is chilling. I enter the MRI room clad for a late fall football game, huddled in a blanket.

Phyllis is fine. She has been told not to move her head. The Valium buzz negates the claustrophobia, but not her ability to scheme. Through all the clanking and buzzing, she's designing a pergola to add to our garden shed. A shady place for the grill with wisteria and a trumpet vine on either end draping over the top.

I hold her hand as I listen. She's relaxed and comfortable. My heart pounds. Courage, calm. How about Valium here? Twenty minutes later, a nurse enters from the hospital.

"Name and date of birth?" she asks.

"Phyllis O'Shea, 9-27-37. That's my maiden name. Phyllis Palladino."

The nurse gently cleanses an area on her arm as she explains, "The dye will highlight any abnormalities. You've done well so far. This won't hurt." She plunges the syringe into one of Phyllis's bulging veins. I look away horrified.

The technician reappears. "Only a little while left."

Phyllis covers her eyes as he slides her back into the tube. He gives me earplugs. I remain in the room and unromantically hold Phyllis's foot. The noise resumes for another twenty-five minutes. Released from the chamber, Phyllis continues her description of the pergola as she sits on the platform waiting for her shoes.

The technician interrupts. With a grave look, he hands me a large brown envelope. "Take this directly to Dr. Sparks. She is waiting for you at the office. We'll cancel the hospital appointment for you."

I'm relieved that the heart is not an issue. What could really go wrong with the brain? I escort Phyllis to the car, her arm in mine, the brown envelope tucked under my other arm. I navigate the familiar, winding, hilly Route 66. I'm untouched by the caprice on the road of life, despite the envelope in the back seat, lurking larger with each mile traveled. Daylight is fading as we burst into the waiting room. The envelope seems larger and heavier. The receptionist bears the envelope to Dr. Sparks. We shuffle into the interior office slightly aware that this could not be good news.

Dr. Sparks holds the tabloid size films up to the light. She turns, and announces, "You have a brain tumor, about the size of a quarter, on the left side of your brain. There is no contrast after the dye was injected, so it doesn't seem to be cancerous. But it has to be removed."

I'm incredulous. Speechless.

"I'll set up an appointment with a surgeon Dr. Rush at St. Peter's in Albany. She's an excellent neurosurgeon. She can evaluate the films and tell you what must happen. Probably surgery to remove the tumor and get you going again."

My swirling brain hears that the tumor can be taken care of. Phyllis hears that someone is about to mess with her brain.

Totally dismayed, Phyllis asks, "How did I get this?"

"It's hard to say," Sparks replies. "Bring the films to Dr. Rush so she can see what's going on."

I grasp Phyllis's arm as we leave the office. She's trembling at the prospect of brain surgery. We fear the worst, hope for the best, lugging the envelope to infinity.

3. Film Reviews

In a little office at St. Peter's Medical annex, our son Dan crams in with Phyllis, me and the brown envelope. Dr. Rush enters and riffs through the content of the envelope to find a couple pictures that tell her what she needs to know. She studies them, and after a few moments says, "It looks like a low-grade tumor. Not cancerous. Its position in the brain makes it inoperable, and risky to biopsy."

I scratch notes on an envelope. *Low grade glioma, grows over time. Can't be cured. Can't be removed.*

Phyllis is relieved. "Well, at least I won't have brain surgery." Brain surgery is more frightening to her than living with and dying relatively young from the benign brain tumor. I stuff my anxiety.

"So, what should we do?" I ask.

The neurosurgeon replies, "I would like to get a better MRI. This one is cloudy. There's a place in Troy with a newer machine that will produce a clearer picture. I trust a doctor there who can give an accurate diagnosis without a biopsy." Rush points to the film. "This cloud indicates a lot of inflammation. We'll reduce the inflammation with a steroid. Then, do another MRI. My secretary will set it up if you don't mind waiting."

"What, then?" I ask still gazing at the cloud that is the tumor.

"I'll review the new information and make some suggestions, maybe radiation, or chemotherapy," Rush replies, removing the films from the light reader.

"What's the prognosis?" Dan asks.

"I don't like to play God, but it's slow growing; maybe six or seven years. Your mother is healthy; that's important. You never know," Rush says as she opens the door to leave.

Six or seven years!

We had retired young from teaching. I'm glad we did that. We have work to do, a life to live. Six or seven years!

The second MRI confirms the first: reduced inflammation but still a cloud, tentacles of the infiltrating tumor compressing the left side of the brain into the right. Possible treatment, low dose whole brain radiation over 2 to 4 weeks. Becky will call from the radiologist's office to set up an appointment.

I want another opinion.

My brother George, a Ph.D. chemist, suggests we go to the Brain Tumor Center in Boston. Meg lives in Boston. I feel comfortable there. The city is manageable. Google provides me with a number to call to begin the next part of the journey. We will confer with the top brain doctors in the world at Massachusetts General Hospital.

Dr. Rush writes a letter to the Boston doctors about Phyllis's condition. Two sentences that stand out for me.

...Her affect is somewhat unusual as she does not appear to be upset regarding this, however this may be her general way of dealing with things. She is awake, alert and oriented.

Phyllis has had a lifetime of dealing with difficult things. The early deaths of her father at 58, mother at 65, and the untimely death of her brother at age 41. She is strong, the other pillar supporting our arch of togetherness.

We will deal with this. Courage. Calm. Patience in the face of disaster. Hopeful in the flickering light.

Before we see Dr. Robert Sage, the radiologist, we are set up for Boston.

I think radiation is drastic for a problem that had only been a nuisance for a little more than a month. Maybe there's something else. I hope the tumor might slink away the way it came, and we can be normal.

I comb the Internet trying to put pieces together. None of the presumed causes of brain tumors apply to Phyllis. No cell phone usage ever, minimal exposure to power lines, microwave only recently enshrined in the kitchen, healthy diet, works out regularly, normal weight. The tumor has not metastasized from another cancer in her body. Phyllis is a happy person. The tumor happened.

I carry the newest pictures in a sleek white envelope. Dr. Sage places the fresh films on a lighted screen. Phyllis and I look over his shoulder at the film. He points out the tumor with its infiltrating lines.

"The midline of the brain has moved a bit. This is difficult," Sage remarks, "I'm glad you're going to Boston; I don't know where to start."

"What's the problem?" I ask as he turns to face us.

"I'm uncomfortable using radiation without first having a biopsy. I would like to know what the Boston group thinks of that; and where to radiate. I'll do whatever they recommend."

We walk out, tired, relieved. Nothing is going to happen yet. The fact that Sage is cautious provides some comfort. We stop at Denny's for a cup of coffee and a sandwich.

Fits of laughter overcome both of us. Nervous laughter evoking tears.

"This is crazy," I say through tears. "One doctor won't operate, and the other doesn't know where to begin with treatment."

The food arrives. We settle down. "Suppose we have six or seven years?" I say. "How should we live it?"

"Just enjoy what we have. I want to be with you. Enjoy Dan and Meg, the family. Have some parties. Nothing extraordinary. Just be with you. Take vacations."

"That sounds like a plan. We can do that."

The sandwiches untouched, we linger over coffee. Uncertain about life. Confident of love. We are together.

22

4. What we have

An abiding love. I had been ordained a Roman Catholic priest for a year. I taught Theology to senior boys at Vincentian Institute in Albany, N.Y. While I was preparing my classroom in September of 1967 an excited senior student rushed into the room and shouted, "Father, there's someone you have to meet." He grabbed me by the arm and dragged me through a corridor jammed with returning students.

At the center of a commotion near the main office, I saw a young nun engaged in lively conversation with a small group of students. I noticed her shapely calves, revealed below the hem of the new habit of the modern nun, accentuated by half high heels. My training forbade me to imagine the light and beautiful body beneath the smart blue shift dress. Within moments, I grasped the warm, firm, confident hand of Sister Mary Sean. "It's nice to meet you," she said.

"Yes! I agree," I said, afraid to reveal any more than a casual interest. A yellow warning light flashed in my mind. Celibacy, a rule of the Roman Catholic Church to establish the space necessary to be a priest, a rule to which I had been bound since ordination, required that I be wary of relationships. Maintaining space in relationships with family, friends, fellow seminarians and especially with women was paramount.

"I'm teaching English to some of these girls. What do you do?" Sister Sean was respectful, and pleasant.

"I'm teaching religion to the senior boys." I replied with slight trepidation maintaining the proper boundary.

We traded glances. Eye contact. Space diminishing, as the student suggested a project that he wanted us to be involved in, a visit to the Jewish synagogue in his neighborhood.

"They're our neighbors. We share a large part of the Bible with them," the student attested, and added impetuously, "I'll talk to the rabbi."

Sister Sean and I laughed together as he rushed off on his mission. "This is going to be interesting," I said.

"Yes," she responded as she breezed into the principal's office.

Having been touched physically with that firm hand shake, by the glance, by the brief mental engagement, by the playful banter, by the light brisk departure, I was on guard.

On leaving the building, I noticed the look of horror on a couple of older nuns as they gazed at the statue of Mary holding a crinkled cigarette butt between her fingers. I just kept walking. A quiet joy welled up in me along with an ominous fear. I liked the interaction with Sister Sean, but also liked serving the Lord as a priest.

A few weeks later, Sister Sean and I accompanied the group of students to the synagogue. During the five-block walk, I talked with the students. I had trouble entering their world. I managed to get side by side with Sister Sean, who had no trouble being part of their world. She was laughing, projecting confidence and excitement about the field trip. After the Rabbi presented a scholarly exegesis of the reading, and concluded the service, the community welcomed us to fellowship with appetizers, music and jubilant dancing. All eyes focused on Sister Sean, who danced and kicked with them.

My world changed rapidly. I began to wonder if I'm in the right calling as I opened my heart a little to Sister Sean on the walk to and from the synagogue, when we passed in the hallways. I was attracted to her.

Through my eight years of study for the priesthood, I managed to stay focused on my goal. Others who began studies with me fell by the wayside. It didn't trouble me that they left. I had no ties to them. I wanted to do God's work as a priest. The seminary years provided tools for the future. At Mater Christi Seminary in Albany, I learned to pray and meditate, while I completed my first two years of college. My next two years I studied at Mount St. Mary's in Emmitsburg, Maryland. I was able to deepen my faith in the traditions of the Church and complete my bachelor's degree in Philosophy. For four more years, I studied Theology at the venerable Theological College at the Catholic University of America in Washington, D.C.

In those four years during the early 1960s, the Church changed. Vatican II, a meeting of all the Catholic bishops in the world shook it up. Fresh thinking scrubbed ancient doctrine and religious practice to present a cleaner, purer vision of faith. Vernacular replaced Latin in rites and ceremonies. Priestly paternalism gave way to lay participation in liturgy and parish governance. Other religions were embraced as separated brothers. Religious sisters transformed from the traditional European habits into modern dress almost overnight. A softening outlook on contraception also seemed to be in the works. Who knew what else might change?

Not celibacy. I was warned by a priest who was trying to determine my fitness for the priesthood at the end of my seventh year of studies. "There has been no change in the law requiring celibacy. You're not entering the priesthood thinking that's going to change."

"No. I accept celibacy," I assured him. "I think it leaves a priest free to concentrate on the Lord's work." I knew my mind, and it was in line with God's. I became another Christ.

Sister Mary Sean said she trusted people more than institutions. While beads were part of the sixties' era, Sister Sean dispensed with her ponderous rosary beads when she replaced the suffocating black habit with modern dress upon her arrival at Vincentian. She changed her name back to her given name and became known as Sister Phyllis O'Shea. Years later, she wrote about her religious experience in an autobiographical sketch:

The family was rather reserved and clannish. I was considered somewhat of an anomaly when I became an out-going, almost frenetically socially active youth. I found being with people to be very rewarding, so I joined all kinds of activities: dramatics, choral, cheerleading, school newspaper, partying, gabbing. I found people fascinating and second only to being with them, I enjoyed reading about them.

At age eighteen, I entered the Religious Sister of Mercy in Albany, N.Y., whose sisters taught me in grade school. All who knew me were stunned, including my family. It was, however, quite practical. This combined many elements of my life: religious, social, educational, and prevented me from having to make a commitment to any one person.

Religious formation, prayer and teaching had become her life. On the fifth anniversary after putting on the religious habit

Sister Mary Sean recited her final vows as a nun with eleven other young women. She became a Spouse of Christ and received a silver wedding band. In a letter to her mother, Sister Sean expressed her profound joy.

> *I'm ready to fly from happiness. I'm so sure this is my life, Mama, that you never need to wonder. I know that it's life with its ups and downs and hardships and frustrations, but for me it's peace and it's joy. I feel that I'm being filled right up with love, and I'm intent on giving and losing myself in God.*

I decided to read different authors to understand relationships and love. I stumbled upon Khalil Gibran's work, *The Prophet*, and focused on the line "Let there be spaces in your togetherness and let the winds of heaven dance between you." This statement was acceptable to my dedication to celibacy.

A month after the synagogue visit, I traveled to Ilion, NY to attend the wake of Sister Phyllis's brother Francis. Francis was well known and loved in his community. Heart complications from rheumatic fever had claimed him in his early forties. The line moved quickly. I approached the grieving Sister Sean. "I'm sorry for your loss." A brief awkward hug. Our bodies touched. I wanted to whisk her away from tears and tragedy. Instead, I drove home with the car full of sisters from the convent who had accompanied me to the wake. It was a joyless, desultory ride.

I anticipated faculty meetings and Mass in the church and convent, times when I might see her, hear her soprano descant soaring above the other voices. I knew she missed her brother. She didn't talk about her loss.

To clear my head, I took a walk around the neighborhood on

an early spring Sunday afternoon. Maple trees were just beginning to bud. Families were enjoying the early spring heat on their porches. I was deep in thought about some issues that had come up that morning. Sister Phyllis disturbed my reverie. "What's wrong, Father?" she asked in her cheerful attractive way.

"Oh, hi. Nothing really," I said trying to avoid the conversation.

"Nothing makes you look so sad. What happens when something makes you sad?" she asked moving closer to my side. We walked together around the several blocks. A space between us as we walked. We greeted families along the way. I felt unburdened as she listened. She shared with me a little about her brother, the rheumatic fever, his years of debilitation. "He wasn't at all well, so he'll be happier where he is," she said, glancing up towards the trees. We concluded the walk with banter about school.

"Maybe we can walk again," I suggested.

"Yes. It was fun!" she responded lithely stepping up to the convent door. A quick turn and a wave as she entered. I waved back. A smile replaced my frown. Someone to talk to.

5. Moving forward

We put on our courage caps. It seems natural. What isn't natural is that we begin to plan our lives around survival. We had taken that for granted. It is not something we had to fight for. The meaning of survival is uncertain. Restoration to wholeness? Bloodied but unharmed? Still standing? Barely able to walk or communicate, yet alive?

The prediction of six or seven years from the not-god surgeon set our objective. We will exceed those years. We will take every step to assure longevity and continue to be for each other. That's why we are together in the first place.

We act for the most part like nothing has changed. We do as we please.

We are reluctant to tell anybody of the tumor that has invaded our life, but word spreads. The family has already joined in our journey as they advised, cooked or baked, and prayed. They send notes and cards of support.

Phyllis and I are determined to honor commitments. We became founding members of the Austerlitz Historical Society in 1988. Served in several offices and now co-chaired the events committee. The second annual Dinner at Old Austerlitz is first on our list. This is a fundraiser which Phyllis and I have put together. For $100 each, up to fifteen people could dine in the splendor of the late 1700 home of Robert Herron. Herron is an antiquarian specializing in antiques from early America. His home is a page from that era. The dinner, either Beef Bourguignon or Salmon, is to be served on antique china, with real silverware, and old glassware. A multi-course meal, soup to nuts. Drinks and fine wine included.

Several men had joined me in training at a local restaurant to serve this exquisite meal. We meet a week before the dinner to review our serving plan. I am not yet 60 years old, and I explain the tumor to my dubious co-workers all in their late sixties.

Herron had been apprised of Phyllis's condition. We had talked of canceling the dinner. Phyllis and I had agreed to go ahead. The tumor is not going to stop life as we know it. The parlor of Herron's old house is abuzz as the five of us men sit together around a blazing fire to discuss our roles to serve the meal.

"First, tell us about Phyllis," one of the men suggests.

I state it simply. "It's a benign, inoperable brain tumor; a condition with which we will have to live, similar to people who live with other conditions such as heart problems."

These guys understand heart conditions. I touch a nerve. "But the brain is different." "Far more complicated than other organs." "Hearts can be operated on, and even replaced with another heart or a small machine." "The brain is very different."

I am not encouraged by their reaction. "We'll do what we have to do," I assure them, and we move on to an unenthusiastic discussion of the dinner.

The second annual dinner at Old Austerlitz is successful. When Phyllis needs to rest, other people fill the gap. She washes the dishes as usual. One plate has a chip. We kick off our shoes at home, exulting before the appointment in Boston on a Thursday in mid-May.

On Tuesday, Phyllis sends an email to the family:

Dear Family,

I'm feeling like a very lucky lady this morning. The diagnosis for my poor brain has been confirmed...an inoperable tumor that can be treated with radiation... I'm no scientist, but finding it makes it possible for me to enjoy life longer. We'll be on our way to the Boston Brain Tumor Clinic...We'll take every course available to us medically. We love you and thank you for your prayers, warmth and support.

Phyllis and Phil

On Wednesday, the eve of the appointment, Phyllis takes time to write to my father:

May 9, 2001

Dear Dad,

Thank you for your prayers and support...you're so strong! It's important to us to know that you're there, a presence no one can replace. Over the years I've again and again wanted to thank you for your family...I feel so privileged to belong. You and Mom have established a "dynasty" that has raised up men and women of strong character and loving hearts; your family values are intact.

Thanks for this lifetime gift; I cherish it.

Much love, Phyllis.

My father, Philip F. Palladino and Phyllis (2003)

6. A Lifetime Gift

One thing occupied my mind on Christmas, 1969. It wasn't mid-night Mass. I planned to visit Sister Phyllis at her home 70 miles away in Ilion, N.Y. during the Christmas break. I'd been a priest a little more than three years. Various projects at V.I. and common concerns pushed us together. We cheered at basketball games. Chaperoned dances. Served on school committees. Counseled the same students. We caroled around the neighborhood with a group of students before Christmas. I loved the proximity. I enjoyed the energy. Sister Phyllis and I managed to keep a discreet space between us during these activities that helped us connect with the young people.

When she invited me to visit her home and meet her relatives after Christmas, I was overjoyed. I wanted to be with her. On Tuesday early evening, after a week-end blizzard, I headed to Ilion. Blinded by the setting sun, I was oblivious to the fact that I was venturing into the Mohawk Valley snow belt. I flew by stacks of melting snow, slightly aware that I was speeding and could get arrested. In a little more than an hour, I arrived at the O'Shea residence shortly after six p.m.

I imagined Sister Phyllis's conversation with her family before my arrival went something like this:

"I invited Father Palladino to come this evening."

"Oh?" Aunt Mary asks.

"I work with him at V.I.; he's a guidance counselor and religion teacher. He is very open minded about things."

33

"You don't say?" Mary comments.

"I have told him a little about you and Bart. He enjoys people and said he would like to meet you."

"It's a tough trip to make with that storm and all," Bart interjects

"Someone special?" Mary asks.

"I suppose so. I'm drawn to him. I never thought I would say that. But he marches to his own drum. He cares about everyone he meets. He's hard to figure. Sometimes I think I am just another one of his friends. Other times, I think I'm someone special. He's very proper. He'll be here in a little while. I'm going to freshen up."

Sister Phyllis pulled me into the quiet living room to introduce me to Aunt Mary and Uncle Bart. They have lived in the family home for over 65 years. The Roman collar peered beneath my chin automatically triggered an immense respect. I'm sure they were curious about the relationship between Father Palladino and their saintly, but precocious, Sister Phyllis. Politeness didn't let them ask. After about fifteen minutes of polite talk and songs played on the piano by Aunt Mary, Sister Phyllis put on her blue pea coat and plaid scarf. "We're going for a walk," she announced neatly tying her furry hat with strings that end in tiny snowballs. Her veil lay on the back of a chair in the living room as if a permanent part of the decor.

We walked uphill on Remington Avenue. A line of brightly lighted Victorian houses, along one side of the street, faced the massive dark Remington Arms factory on the other side. Sister Phyllis explained the street. "There was a magnificent view of the valley when Grand Daddy built our house. Then they built the factory. No more view. Just noise and shots to test rifles. My whole family worked there. I escaped to the convent."

Near the end of the street, a flurry of snowflakes moved us closer. She slipped her hand into mine, and then into my warm coat pocket. I felt a surge of desire. Communication was difficult. We had spent two years avoiding intimate conversation. In a disconnected way, we thought out loud "What if...?"

What if we had met when we were younger? What if we hadn't chosen to work for the Church? What if we had not pledged our lives to celibacy?

Celibacy. We were expected by family, friends, and the Church, to abide by those vows. People committed to the religious life or the priesthood do not change course. Priests do not fall in love. Period. If one found that happening, it was important to avoid the near occasion of sin. "Our relationship is something I never expected," I said with hesitation.

"I never thought about being in any relationship," she replied. "I'm not sure what ours is. You move so freely among people."

"You must know that you're different from others," I said.

"You say that now. I don't see that all the time. You belong to everybody. Whatever you do seems to be done equally for people and me included," she said squeezing my hand in my pocket.

Feeling deflated, I stated, "But you're special. I care about you deeply."

"I'm glad you care," she said as she tightened her grip in my pocket. "I want the best for you. I care about you too."

"What if we were free to be for each other?" I asked.

"Could you settle for that?" she replied. "That's impossible. You're too dedicated; and you have your whole family to deal with."

"If settling is the right word, I could be for you. I don't know what they'd think if I suddenly changed direction," I answered shivering at the thought of announcing to my family any change in my life. I squeezed her hand very hard.

At the front steps, she asked, "So, what's next?"

"I'm not sure. I have an idea of a direction I want to go. It will take time. Time to practice courage," I suggested as I again shivered, extracting warmth from her hand.

"Right!" she laughed. The warmth of her hand. Enveloping, cozy snow. Peace. All embraced us.

About one and a half years after this conversation, I broke the news to my parents that I was going to leave the priesthood and get married. My mother, despite an attack of high blood pressure, was happy to hear that Sister Phyllis was my love. My Dad encouraged me. "Don't do anything for us. It's your life. It's important that you be happy," he counseled. His words dispelled any doubt. A lifetime gift for both of us.

Phil and Phyllis, wedding day, June 12,1972.

7. Maybe it's something else

We set out to Boston early in the day on Thursday. The white envelope with the latest MRI, letters from Sparks and Rush, are packed in my briefcase.

I feel confident that the doctors here can help. Confidence overshadows dread. It even eliminates brain tumors. We lock hands and enter the Brain Tumor Center through glass doors.

Signs welcome us. A receptionist points us in the right direction. The wait is too short for me to fill in all the questions on the clipboard. There is time later.

Dr. David Larsen, a neurological intern from California, puts Phyllis through the paces: balance, precision, comprehension. No problem. I'm elated with each success. I think that Phyllis does better on these tests than I could.

About three quarters of the way through the examination, Larsen instructs Phyllis, "I want you to remember three words: ball, pen and table." She repeats them. I forget the words almost immediately. Larsen proceeds with more tests. *Touch your nose with your right index finger. Squeeze my hand. Walk on a line heel to toe.* A full five minutes of questions, answers, instructions and responses. He hands Phyllis a clipboard. "Write a complete sentence, subject, predicate and object."

Phyllis pauses, writes, "I am remembering three words, ball, pen and table." Her hand writing is legible as she had always written.

39

Amused, Larsen asks the last question, "What are the three words I told you to remember?"

"I am remembering ball, pen, and table," Phyllis proudly announces, as if to say, *See, there's nothing wrong with me.* I tend to agree. I think maybe it's not what it looks like on the films; maybe it's something else, curable, an infection.

The head of the brain tumor division, Dr. Bremer, reviews the films as we relax in the black vinyl upholstered chairs. "Could it not be a tumor?" I ask when he looks up from the films.

"It's a tumor. So far it has had a minimal effect. It can be treated, but not cured." He gives his lecture about brain tumors. "There are about 120 kinds of brain tumors, some malignant, others benign: some are primary-they arise in the brain: and others, secondary metastasizing from another cancer in the body. You do not have cancer; this is primary non-malignant." Bremer is certain, except, "I don't know what kind of tumor it is. Each kind of tumor has several different treatments. We need a biopsy to know what to treat."

Dr. Rush in Albany considered a biopsy a great risk, so I ask, "Is that safe to do?"

"We do them every day. It's an outpatient procedure; less than twenty-four hours," he assures us. He looks sternly at Phyllis. "You should take no more than two weeks to decide on a biopsy."

No more than two weeks. A warning, not a suggestion. The Boston guys, the real experts want a biopsy. Do we play it safe with Dr. Rush who suggested whole brain radiation as the treatment? Or go with the experts at Boston? Or do we get a third opinion? We discuss this on the way home. We want the best treatment available. Rush offered only one, but the radiologist would not guess at where to radiate. To walk out on the Boston doctors seems crazy. Doing nothing is not an option.

"If it needs to be done, we should do it," Phyllis says.

On Monday morning, I call the Brain Tumor Center to set up the biopsy. On May 31, Phyllis and I report to Mass General for pre-admission for the outpatient biopsy. Blood work, physical. Health care proxy, a piece of paperwork from nowhere. Phyllis entrusts her health care decisions to me if she is incapacitated. It's only a biopsy. They do them every day. We'll get through this nightmare and move on with life.

8. Our Boston Marathon

Meg's apartment is in Jamaica Plain at the end of the Massachusetts Transit, or the T, Boston's commuter rail. It's easier to take the T to and from the hospital than to drive. We stay in her apartment on the night of May 31. Meg has a deep meaningful conversation with her Mother that night. "This is fun having you here; I wish we had more time together," Meg tells her.

"We'll get together after this business at the hospital tomorrow, I'll be okay," Phyllis assures her.

"Okay, sleep well. Good night; love you." Meg embraces her mom, and then hugs me, "Good night, Dad. You know how to get there, right?"

"Yes. We'll be fine." I give Meg one more hug and then sink into the low bed, a box spring and mattress on the floor. "So, are you okay?" I ask Phyllis as I hold her under the blanket.

"It's nerve racking, but I put you in charge today. You'll do a good job," she jokes, betraying only courage. Affectionate touches beneath the covers, several short kisses and a big long one. "I need my rest," Phyllis says.

Sirens of the city. Images of the day. Dreams of happiness on the other side of a nightmare. Second thoughts. Sleep eludes me.

Before the sun hits the pavement, Phyllis and I march down the hill to the T. Hand in hand, we step onto the train, a

43

tubular abyss. The train lurches forward humming and clacking along the rails. Lights flicker. Ads on the walls fly by: *Realty U, Toyota, Boston Garden, Red Sox*. Brakes squeal, *Roxbury*. Clack, clack-clack. Squeal, *Ruggles*. The content of the car changes almost completely, and again at Chinatown. *Downtown Crossing*. Screech. Transfer. We scurry with a small crowd to the Red line outbound. Plenty of seats, a fresh group of travelers and two stops to *Charles/MGH*. When I plant my feet on the concrete platform, perhaps the last semblance of certainty in life, something is different. Planning, future, hope, faith dissolved in that T. Destiny has taken over.

We arrive at the hospital at around 8 a.m. Phyllis's fingers, her whole body like the Pillsbury Doughboy, swelled by the Decadron prescribed by Dr. Rush. "She has to take those rings off," the receptionist insists. The rings do not budge. An attendant tries soap to no avail. The secretary brings a cutter. Success. I take the mangled eight-dollar fourteen karat gold wedding ring that has bound us for twenty-nine years and slide it onto my left pinky, next finger to my ten-dollar ring. The mother's ring with its aquamarine and sapphire stones joins Phyllis's wedding ring on my pinky. The severed edges cut into me. It's okay. Bravery resides in Phyllis as she mounts the gurney, on a journey unknown. I hug her, "You'll be okay. I'll take care of the rings."

The nurses affix an apparatus to her head to stabilize it during an MRI and the entire procedure. "This is my Easter bonnet!" Phyllis jokes.

"No, this is to keep your head stable during the biopsy!" the orderly rejoins sternly.

44

"Oh!" she replies meekly to that overwhelming piece of redundant information. The fact that she remembers this exchange heartens me in the days ahead.

The fear that I had as I stepped off the T becomes reality. Dr. Baker calls me in the waiting room. "Your wife began to have seizures when I pulled the third strand from the tumor. It's going to take time, and you won't be going home today. We have to stop the seizures." Not what I want to hear. The good news that the samples are not cancerous is some comfort. I find the non-sectarian chapel. When I was ten years old, I prayed for the New York Giants to beat the Brooklyn Dodgers. My prayer was answered instantly with a walk-off home run by Bobby Thompson. Almost thirty years into our marriage, fifty years after that home run, we need a miracle. In the quiet, I don't pray. No whisper of "God help me." No desperate propitiation. No bargaining for a different outcome. I choose not to pray. I center my thoughts on how to meet the current challenge. I summon up courage to walk. To speak with confidence. To enjoy what we have.

9. The prayer dilemma

Phyllis and I both enjoyed growing up Catholic. We cherished the schooling in our younger years. Phyllis was a choir girl, endowed with a beautiful voice. The Sisters in charge of her elementary school loved her and her beautiful soprano that soared above the others. Encouragement from these Sisters of Mercy were the incentive for her to enter the convent.

I was privileged to be an altar boy. Almost daily, but Sundays especially, I appeared as the good boy serving the priest, swinging the censer, creating the heavenly aroma that seemed to entrance old ladies into a deep prayerful stupor. Life was good.

I had to go to confession occasionally, but there were points for this if I appeared to be especially contrite. I said a decade of the rosary at the communion rail. Perhaps someone would notice. I couldn't really spend too much time on my knees, lest someone wonder, "What did he do?"

My list of sins was simple and brief. Mostly disobedience to my parents or arguing with my brothers or sisters. If I had impure thoughts or worse, I found Father Connally in the dark confessional, spoke quickly, before he even woke up. He might have heard the last part, "I disobeyed my mother three times." "Say three hail Mary's" was his usual penance. Then he gave me absolution and I was good to go. I often thought that I should add adultery to my list of sins to see if the three hail Mary penance was consistent. However, for most of my early childhood and teenage years, I had no idea what adultery was. A sin, yes, but how do you do it?

Ten years into our marriage, Phyllis and I bring our children, Dan and Meg, to religious events at Christmas and Easter when we feel like it just to keep in touch. "What do we keep in touch with?" my son Dan asks.

"We keep in touch with our roots," I say, "but we believe differently now than we did then. You don't need to know all the things Mom and I were taught." The tale told me when I was young no longer resonates in my heart. It has become a curious literary object that guides my attitude towards the people I meet. The virtues of religion, such as caring and compassion leave an indelible mark. I understand that these are human qualities that all people regardless of faith practice to some degree.

Phyllis and I find God in each other. We live for each other. Our wills unite in our mutual love. The relationship is all that matters in daily life.

At every funeral for an aunts and uncles, even my own mother and father, I deliver the eulogy. I speak of faith. Quote the Bible. I use phrases like "we were taught," or "we were brought up to believe." I speak of my own father as the God we all seek too far off. The space between us and God is an embrace, a kiss away. I don't talk about being united with a loved one in heaven but refer to the deceased as being still with us. I don't have to explain. No one parses the language of eulogies. The words speak to the hearts of the listeners. They believe what they want to believe.

In my quiet reflection, I know the season to enjoy what we have.

48

10. Beyond the disbelief

The seizures abate late that night. Dr. Baker dressed in his green operating fatigues and cap moves around the dimly lighted ICU like it's his home. He leads me through a maze of machines and tubes, through crowded openings.

"There's nothing going on that I haven't seen before," he says confidently, his stethoscope slung over his shoulder. "Ninety-eight percent of biopsies go with no problem. Your wife, unfortunately, is in the other two per cent. We'll find the right medication." His confidence is reassuring. "I have to talk with the epilepsy doctors. Visit a while. She'll recover."

My stomach churns. I take a deep breath to calm myself. We will get back. I hold Phyllis's raw puffy hands. I press my cheek to her bloated face. I stroke her cropped hair that is like the hair she revealed at the drive-in so many years ago when we first embraced to ward of the chill of the evening. I felt her bony arms beneath her trench coat and thought how wonderful it was to hold her. I relive that moment. I carefully avoid twisted tubes as I wrap my arms around her and whisper, "I love you; I'll take care of you."

When the long-awaited dawn comes, the monitors reveal good news. Her lips move, a twitch, seizure activity. She's out of it. I adjust my position and find her swollen right hand, the one without the tubes. It's dry and rough. I apply some lotion.

Dr. Baker with his team of surgeons checks on his patient. "Dr. Bremer will discuss Phyllis's condition with the pathologists to figure out what's next," he says. He checks her puffy legs. I later find out that he's concerned about blood clots. The team leaves.

Phyllis wakes up when Meg comes in. Meg blanches at the sight of her fallen mother. She climbs into the bed next to her, and they hold each other amid the tubes and needles. They're both frightened, holding back tears, but brave as they communicate love amid fear and uncertainty.

Meg was acquainted with trauma in college at Simon's Rock when a troubled student shot and killed a student and a teacher. A third person was wounded. Meg joined the crisis team during the following semester to help her fellow students deal with fallout from the shooting. It's different when it's your own mother who is in trouble. She's you.

Dan arrives from Albany shortly after Meg. He manages to give his Mom a big hug in the middle of the embrace that engulfs Phyllis and Meg. He's terrified. I calmly explain the situation as told to me by the medical team. He nods but concentrates his glance on his Mom.

Phyllis tries to speak, then decides to keep silent and simply follow the conversation, a spectator to her own life. She takes some lunch. We banter about nothing, avoiding any topics that might involve her in the frustration of speaking.

Elaine, a Physical Therapist, pokes her head into the room. "We'll get you up tomorrow. How about that?" Phyllis responds with a nod and a crooked smile and soon dozes off. We take our leave, so she can rest. The nurses will do their job. As we ride the T to Meg's apartment, Meg asks, "When do you think she'll be better?"

"The doctor thinks there will be improvement in a few days," I answer.

"How do you deal with this?" Meg asks me. "You seem so calm!"

"We always practiced courage and calm, especially when we first met. It was important. That's what I'm doing."

"How?" she asks.

"You just do it. That's all. It takes practice. We'll get her out of here soon. She will recover." I'm irked but I dare not cry. I must lead them through this.

Dan talks about the day he, Phyllis and I met at Dr. Rush's office in Albany. "That was a tough day. Mom didn't want anyone messing with her brain," he says.

"Yeah! We had to figure a way to treat it. Mom is in that unlucky two percent," I say staring ahead at the station sign.

"It's hard to figure out the right thing to do," Dan reassures me. "We depend on these guys." He swallows hard, still holding back tears.

"Tomorrow will be better," I assure him.

When I arrive at the hospital the next morning, the team of nurses is buzzing. One of them corners me. "You have to talk to your wife. She got out of bed last night to go to the bathroom. She should have called the night nurse. She unhooked all the tubes first," the nurse explains.

I'm elated to hear this. "Yes, but that's dangerous. We will have to restrain her, so this won't happen again," she warns.

Phyllis abhors restraints. She smiles a crooked smile as I walk through the door. "Everybody's talking about you. They're worried that you might fall when you get out of bed," I admonish with a touch of glee.

"I'm b-b-b-better t-t-t-now," she says.

"Call the nurse when you need to go to the bathroom. It's their job." I have a feeling that my words are useless. She never did, nor does she intend to depend on anyone to move around. I give her a big hug. "Today, the Physical Therapist wants to get you walking."

"It's about t-t-t-time...about time."

As I talk with nurses and staff, I learn about aphasia, the lack of ability to speak. The speech problem becomes more pronounced as Phyllis becomes more alert. When a nurse comes in to change the IV bags, and asks, *Date of birth.* I reply "9-27-37." Walking is less of a problem. Although she is unsteady, Phyllis does what P.T. Elaine requests, and makes a face. *There, I did that. Now what?* After the walk she needs to rest. The aide comes in and straps the pressure leggings on to prevent blood clots.

"How long will she need those?" I ask.

"Until she walks a lot," the aide answers. She defines a lot as about five times a day. Five walks a day becomes a goal. We can control something.

52

11. Winning the Race

After Phyllis rests from the therapy, we start despite slight twitches of seizure activity on the right side of her face. I help her out of bed. She prefers my arm to the walker. With my free hand, I roll the IV stand, a staff for the journey. We walk to the nurses' station silently except for my whispered encouragement and caveats. The nurses and aides smile at the progress. "It's good to see you up and about," one says. Phyllis flashes a crooked triumphant smile.

"Five times a day. This is two," I proclaim. We pass the station, do a loop around the neurological area leaving many workers in the dust. A careful tumble into bed completes the lap. "Meg will be here after work. We'll do a third when she gets here. Rest up." Phyllis curls up amid the tubes. I don't put the pressure leggings back on. While she rests, I walk to the nurses' station to see if there is anything new on the charts. A plan for treatment. A date for release. Nothing.

I read a history book, *Constantine's Sword,* about the effects of the reign of Constantine on the entire history of Europe. The use of religion to achieve power. The use of power in the name of religion. It reinforces my latest thinking about the Church and the God effect. I wish I had brought something lighter. I fall asleep. Meg finds me an hour later in the immense solarium close to the elevators. "Relaxing?" she says with her cheerful smile.

I look up groggy, "Hi, glad to see you. You got out early."

"Yes. How's Mom?" she asks.

"We're waiting for you to do the third run. Tomorrow, we'll do five," I excitedly tell her.

Meg's enthused. "Great, let's go" she says yanking me from the deep sofa. We rush to Phyllis's room. Phyllis, sitting in a chair, brightens at the sight of Meg. She tries to respond. Words are not there. We know that she's feeling better. We help her to her feet. Phyllis holds on to my arm. Meg supports the other side. The tethered I.V. follows. Sunlight fills the solarium on this early June day. While we rest in the sun, Meg looks over her mother's wounds. The patch on her head. Abrasions caused by the brace applied for the operation. Black and blue marks from technicians searching for a good vein into which to pump fluid. Swollen legs a by-product of medications.

"We want to get you home where you can get better," Meg says. "You've been here too long."

"Thursday or Friday might be the day," I guess. "The social worker will be around to make sure you will be going to a place that's good."

Phyllis's face conveys incredulity. I interpret her sounds and gestures to mean *What do they mean good? You're going to be there, that's all that matters.* I allay her indignation. "I know it'll work. You've only been here a few days, and you were strong when you came in. That's why the walking is so easy." I'm comforting myself. I can't think of any other way to wholeness for Phyllis, the family and for me.

After a while, we help her to her feet and return to her room for dinner. Phyllis manages to eat the sandwich with little trouble. She devours the vanilla ice cream after I remove the cap.

She puts the tea bag into the cup of hot water. Recovery is happening. The IV bag is replenished after I give the birth date "9-27-37."

Phyllis turns in for the night early after a day of strides forward. Meg and I inform the nurses that we are leaving. They are concerned that Phyllis might wander. A discussion ensues whether to restrain her. I suggest that they watch her, but not restrain her. They decide to do it anyway that night after I leave. Phyllis lets me know about that the next morning. Suddenly, she's speaking. "They tied me up. I hate it here. When are we going h-h-h-home?"

"They shouldn't do that to you. You're talking," I point out. Cleaned up and ready for the day, Phyllis is anxious to continue the race. P.T. is scheduled for early afternoon. The social worker will be around this evening. A full day. The nurse comes in with a handful of pills: anti-convulsants, pain relievers, Zantac, all new since the biopsy. "9-27-37," I respond to the nurse's question.

We begin the first lap by way of the nurses' station. We wave, expecting confetti. A post-it flies off the bulletin board. We're around the track once, and anxious to go one more time before lunch. Phyllis's face contorts into a seizure. I immediately lead her to her chair. Phyllis sits until after lunch. About one o'clock, P. T. comes. Leg stretches, arms stretches, and a walk. Elaine is impressed with Phyllis's efforts. "She's getting stronger. A little shaky. I'll prescribe a cane for her to take home." Home, the magic word. A cane, Phyllis rolls her eyes. I see the cane as a temporary solution to Phyllis's unsteadiness. "Will we get to full recovery?" I ask.

"Phyllis came to us with lots of problems," P.T. states.

"No," I retort. "We took the subway to the hospital last Friday. She was walking, talking and laughing. There were no problems. I want to take her home as soon as possible."

"I'll meet with the team and see when that can happen," Elaine promises as she completes the walk with Phyllis.

12. The Finish Line

Five laps a day around the track. A cheering crowd. A race to freedom. A final exit. Mary Sunder, the social worker, expedites the discharge with a strong recommendation that Phyllis should spend a few weeks in rehab. "I'll take her home. She'll be fine," I argue.

"Well she has some serious needs," Sunder responds. "Balance, personal skills, and speech for starters. Her medications need monitoring. Weekly blood tests."

It's an outline for a tragedy. Anything can happen. Phyllis squirms, attempts to speak and then withdraws from the conversation. I take a deep breath. I stand up straighter. I know that Phyllis and I can navigate recovery. We need time together. "Phyllis is strong. She does four walks a day plus the walk with the therapist. I can do that at home."

"But what about the other things?" Sunder counters.

"We have plenty of time. We'll deal with them," I exclaim.

"Phyllis is scheduled for release on Friday. I'll write up my recommendation. You seem determined to do what you want," Sunder says.

Phyllis smiles and claps simultaneously. "We're going h-h-home!"

The day after the social worker's visit, Dr. Larsen shows up. He's been monitoring Phyllis's progress on the screens near the nursing station. "Many people who come here take care of everything at once: the biopsy, the treatment and rehab," he tells me.

"What's the recommended treatment for Phyllis?" I ask anticipating his answer.

"When the team decides, we'll be recovering at home. You have my phone number," I tell him with an air of finality.

Larsen sets up a radiologist consultation for us before we leave on Friday. The conversation with these doctors makes radiation seem about as easy as eating a sandwich. Just brush off the crumbs and you're good to go. I don't like it. It's her brain after all.

Phyllis eagerly walks with me and the therapist. "I hope you don't have stairs to climb at home," Elaine says. "They could be a problem."

"Uh-huh'" I mumble. I don't mention that I had already tried Phyllis on the stairs next to the elevator. After three tenuous steps, she wanted to do more. I had to coax her to come down.

"I'm recommending a cane for Phyllis to use for balance. Rehab could help a lot," Elaine insists.

"We'll be okay," I reassert.

She gives Phyllis a lesson on cane-walking which Phyllis disdains. Phyllis leans instead on Elaine.

A checkout nurse comes in at 11:00 a.m. on Friday. She runs down an excruciating list of Phyllis's symptoms, followed by a recitation of medications with exact times and dosages. Then come the recommendations and suggestions from the staff that I must sign so everyone knows the staff's efforts. Consult with the radiologist. Done. Signed. Consult with the therapist who issued a cane and recommends PT. Signed. Consult with social worker who recommends a rehabilitation facility. "Husband refuses service." I hesitate, peeved at the insinuation that I am ignoring the social worker's advice to the detriment of Phyllis needs. I sign expansively like John Hancock on the Declaration of Independence. I know what will work. A rehab facility will not work. Phyllis asks to sign the final release page. With little effort, she writes "Phyllis". Near perfect handwriting. Then with near perfect handwriting, "Pallalala...."

"Stop!" I say, "Write 'dino," She does.

"It'll get better," the nurse declares. "I'll get a wheelchair." Phyllis plops into the wheelchair. The shunned cane in her lap. She smells the finish line. I take the stairs, streak down the six flights, complimenting myself on my ability to beat the elevator.

"We're going home," I sing to everyone within earshot. I know that whatever shape Phyllis is in she'll get better. By the time I pull up towards the entrance, the nurse has pushed Phyllis closer to the driveway. I stop near them; the nurse locks the chair and Phyllis struggles impatiently from the chair, slightly tripping on the foot rests. She falls into the front seat followed by the cane which she accepts begrudgingly from the nurse.

"Thanks for your help," I wave to the nurse. Phyllis fumbles to free herself from the cane, fighting it and then motioning for me to put it in the back. She's free. We're free, off to pick up Meg at her apartment. Victory.

13. Homeward Bound

Our new journey has tension like the escape to Mount Greylock in our younger days. Mount Greylock, Massachusetts, 35 miles from Albany, was a place of refuge where Phyllis and I could be together without the trappings of religious garb. We could talk, laugh, and play far from the eyes and ears of people who would be circumspect of a priest and a nun alone together, obviously on a date. Then we were anxious and uncertain. On a journey in a forbidden relationship. Today, we are anxious to begin the journey together to recovery. Uncertain of the treatment. Uncertain about time. Certainty only in each other.

I ride shotgun as Meg snakes through the early afternoon traffic to the Mass Pike. She glances toward the rearview mirror trained on her Mom and presses the gas. Miles fly by. Rest areas are a blur. All under construction like us.

By mid-afternoon, our breezy, sunny home welcomes us. We check the rudbeckia and hollyhocks. The warm swimming pool is green with algae. Tree swallows occupy one of the birdhouses. Our new tent stands high and dry in the yard, awaiting an expedition. The weekend of the biopsy had originally been planned as a camping trip to Camden, Maine with my brother George and his wife Theresa. Phyllis peers curiously into the tent and asks, "Is someone camping here?"

"No, that was for our trip to Maine. George and Theresa visited you in the hospital instead," I reply.

"Oh, I forgot," she says.

Meg helps us settle on the porch. No nurses. Songs of sparrows and cardinals replace the clatter of the hospital. The team of care givers has shrunk and will be reduced to one. When Meg returns to Boston on Sunday, my head spins with the responsibility. Be cheerful. Be vigilant. Supply comfort. Dispense medications. A daily routine. Cook. Clean the house. Walk. Mary, my sister, suggests a method for organizing the pills and reminds me that there is leeway to dispense them close to the prescribed times. "Use little plastic cups marked with the hours and pills," she tells me. I mark six cups with the hours: 6 a.m., noon, 3 p.m., 6 p.m., bedtime, midnight. I also write the pills and dosage on the side. Decadron, a steroid that reduces inflammation is in four cups but is alone in the midnight cup.

Mary, an operating room nurse. My sister Jean, a former nurse. My sister-in-law Patsy, a nurse with a cardiologist in Troy. Our reinforcements arrive on Sunday with cheer. Pasta and salads. Patsy notices the pill cups arranged on the counter. "It looks like you have everything under control."

"Maybe, but that one every six hours," I complain, "we don't have time to sleep. How do I get this changed?"

"You'll have to see a neurologist. Did the Boston doctors refer you to one?" Mary asks.

"No. We'll see a radiologist tomorrow," I say looking out the window. I don't know what comes next!" The lack of direction causes consternation. After giving a mountain of advice, they leave. Phyllis decides to take control. She hides the cane in the linen closet several rooms away. Within minutes, she trips on the old uneven floor. "You don't want the cane?" I ask as I help her up.

62

"No, I'm fine," she insists.

"You've got to watch her more carefully," Meg admonishes. "Mom can get into trouble."

"Yes! This is new territory," I acknowledge feeling very inadequate.

After a sleep interrupted by pill dosage, we leave at 7:30 a.m. for our appointment in Albany with Dr. Sage. The receptionist greets us. "I called your house, but there was no answer," she says apologetically. "Dr. Sage was injured in a car crash Saturday. He's in critical condition."

"Oh! I'm sorry to hear that," I say concerned for Sage's condition, but chagrined that we had come all this way for nothing.

"Dr. Morrison, an associate, is available. He'll see you," she says pointing to the chairs in the waiting room. After a short wait, we enter Morrison's office.

"Thanks for seeing us, doctor," I say as I extend my hand to shake his. "This is Phyllis, my wife. Did the Boston Brain Tumor Center send any information?"

"We haven't heard from them," he responds. Morrison listens as I recount our conversations with Dr. Rush and Dr. Sage, the pursuit of a second opinion, the biopsy, the seizures, the medications. Morrison promises to get in touch with the Boston doctors.

He then reviews the medications. "Let's cut out the mid-night Decadron. Three times a day is fine. You'll get more sleep," he says to Phyllis. "It will also reduce your appetite."

As soon as we get home, I throw out the mid-night cup.

With no clear direction, I call several neurologists, practically begging for help. "The doctor will get back to you." "The practice is closing this week." "Epilepsy usually surfaces in childhood, so we only deal with those cases."

Feeling very alone, I call the Boston Brain Tumor Center. A receptionist passes me over to the nurse who tries to reassure me, "The doctor will be in touch." A day passes. I call Dr. Baker's office for information. Still nothing other than a reminder to come in several days to have the stitches removed.

"Do we have to drive back to Boston to have the stitches removed?" I ask.

"If there is someone locally who will do it, that would be fine," the receptionist replies. I cancel the stitch removal in Boston for an appointment with Dr. Sparks. Another day passes. The voice on the phone says. "We have received a call and a fax from Dr. Bremer's office, regarding Phyllis Palladino. Dr. Spinner can see her next Wednesday at one. Can you make it?"

"We'll be there," I say.

Finally, something is happening.

14. Doctor Spinner

"Who is Doctor Spinner?" I ask.

"The only doctor between New York City and Canada who treats brain tumors," the voice on the phone replies.

My heart skips a beat. "Great! Thank you. We'll see you Wednesday."

"Bring the latest MRI films for the doctor to review," the voice prescribes.

Phyllis and I shop and walk for another week. Dr. Sparks removes the stitches on Tuesday, which is more than two weeks after the biopsy. She encourages us, "You're doing okay. Keep at it. I've never met Dr. Spinner, but he has a wonderful reputation."

We arrive that Wednesday at Albany Medical Center, ten days after Phyllis was released from Mass General. My wallet is bulging with Phyllis's insurance cards, her ID, and anything else that was important in her wallet.

A prescription for blood work has been ordered by the doctor whom we have yet to meet. "Name and birth date?" the phlebotomist asks.

I respond immediately, "Phyllis Palladino. 9-27-37."

After her blood is drawn, nurse Betty leads us to a smaller waiting room, where she takes Phyllis's pulse, blood pressure and temperature. I rattle off the medications, "Dilantin, Depakote, Decadron."

Nurse Betty quickly jots the information into a computer. "Dr. Spinner will be in shortly. She's running late today. Lots of patients. She's been on maternity leave." I recall *he has a wonderful reputation.*

Phyllis says, "How wonderful! And she came back. For me?"

"Yes. You could say that," Betty responds as she leaves and closes the door.

Phyllis reaches over and opens the door a bit. "I need air."

A soft swish of a pants suit followed by fingernails clicking on the door jamb heralds Dr. Spinner's arrival. "Hi, I'm Dr. Spinner. Can I come in?" she asks as she pokes her curly blond head into the room. I grasp her extended hand, not wanting to let go. It reminds me of the hand that Phyllis extended thirty-five years ago at Vincentian Institute. Warm, confident, assertive.

"I forgot the films," I say.

"That's okay, I have information from the pathologists in Boston. How do you feel Mrs. Palladino?" Spinner asks Phyllis a lot of questions, does some neurological tests, talks about treatment possibilities. "The two best pathologists in the world can't agree on the status of the tumor, whether it is active or stable. Clinically, you seem to be very good. I see you're still having some focal seizures," referring to some twitches around

Phyllis's mouth that I thought were not unusual. "The blood test indicates that the Dilantin is not at a therapeutic level; we will adjust that and see if it helps. The rest of the blood work appears to be normal. We should watch out for blood clots in your legs, a side effect of these tumors."

Phyllis takes it all in. "How's the baby?" she asks.

"He's doing fine," Spinner gushes. "He's getting used to life. I miss him."

Phyllis's confidence builds. A few weeks later, the procedure repeats. Blood work. Tap on the door, "May I come in?" The handshake. "You seem better. The seizure activity is under control. Clinically you are doing fine. We will monitor the tumor with MRIs. There is no cure. At some point treatment will be necessary. We'll decide on that down the road."

Phyllis is elated. No treatment. "I'm going to put you on the map," she informs the doctor.

I feel good about Spinner's approach and Phyllis's response.

Despite Spinner's pronouncements of no cure, Phyllis works to put Spinner on the map. A week after the visit, we shop the summer clearance at K-Mart. Although the shopping cart gives Phyllis stability, it doesn't prevent her from bumping the racks and merchandise stacked in the aisles. As I peruse the outdoor rugs in the lawn and garden section, I realize the shopping cart is parked near me. Phyllis is gone. I stretch tall like a periscope, peering over the racks. No Phyllis. My heart pounds. My head pounds. Do I wander and search? Do I call out? Have her paged? I freeze where I am. *Where the hell is she?* The cart moves. My nightmare dissolves.

"Where were you?" I ask.

"I was testing myself," she says. "You've been glued to me almost forever. I needed to see if I could do something on my own. I walked around, and I came back. I can do it."

"That's great. Let me know the next time," I respond holding back my anxiety. I place a straw hat in the basket as my present for my sixtieth birthday, and as a monument to her gritty courage. I remember that whenever the hat blows off as I mow.

On the way home, Phyllis asks, "Whom shall we invite to your birthday party?"

"My brothers and sisters, and Pat. Maybe some others to make it special," I suggest.

"Who, neighbors? Friends?" she asks desiring to please me.

"How about my first cousins? Most of them have never been here," I say.

"It's your birthday. Maybe your cousin Margaret will come." My cousin Margaret knew Phyllis over forty years ago when they both entered the convent. Margaret left the convent after about six months to study nursing.

Although my sixtieth birthday is special, I'm not happy. As hopeful as I am that a cure will be found, I am haunted by the fact that there is no cure for Phyllis's condition. I know that my sixties will be fraught with change, and not for the better. I summon up optimism, for the party, for the family, for Phyllis.

Margaret comes to the party and reminisces with Phyllis about the convent years. Margaret was elated when Phyllis and I got married. "My friend Phyllis Jane married my cousin Philip John. The P.J.s." Margaret whispers encouragement to me, "Phyllis seems good, still laughing and fun as I remember her."

I cut the cake, buoyed by my supportive siblings and cousins. Good things happen during the ensuing weeks. Phyllis gets into that heavy book, "Constantine's Sword."

"This is different from what we were taught in grade school," she observes as she looks up from the book. "I thought there was a vision that everyone saw at that bridge. A miracle."

She's referring to an alleged vision that portended the historic victory for Constantine at Milvian Bridge in the year 312. The book dismisses the vision as a legend perpetrated by Constantine himself years after the battle, a far different version from what was taught in the Catholic schools.

"Yes, this book is more accurate," I say.

"It goes along with what we were studying with our friends before we went to Boston," Phyllis recalls, slowly turning a page.

"Do you think we'll get back to the group?" I ask.

"Let's give it some time," she suggests. "When I can talk better."

At the end of the summer, a fresh MRI reveals no change. "No change is good," Nurse Betty reminds us as she updates Phyllis's medications. Spinner enters the room and extends her warm hand. She does some neurological evaluations. "You are doing well. Walking and talking have improved. The blood work is in order. I can't rule out the possibility of a seizure in the future. If it lasts longer than 15 minutes call the rescue squad."

"A seizure could be finished before they get there," I say.

"And that's okay, they won't mind not having to do anything, so call them," Spinner assures me.

My 60th birthday: Phyllis, Dan, Meg and Me

70

15. Nothing Extraordinary

Phyllis and I settle into a routine. A daily walk around our property several times equals a mile. We prepare meals together. She does the laundry, and I do the dishes as we had done while we worked at Chatham High School. We switch every couple of weeks to allay boredom. We watch the news. Entertain friends.

We continue our active membership in the Austerlitz Historical Society (AHS) by serving on the events committee. We are co-chairs of Autumn in Austerlitz (A in A) a festival that Phyllis had started several years before to raise funds for the Austerlitz Historical Society. A in A looms on the first Saturday of fall. In the middle of doctor's visits, and on-again off-again aphasia, we refuse to pass the whole thing back to the Society. That would concede that life has changed, a concession that we don't want to make. "How do we want to get this done?" I ask Phyllis.

"Let's have a dessert party. That's why we built the porch. We'll make two big trifles and invite the people in charge of each activity." There's no hesitation on her part. She knows how to get it done.

The committee chairpersons show up, plus a few extras. Fifteen people. The chairpersons give their reports while I take notes. Phyllis announces, "We seem to be on track. Very good. Time for dessert." Like ants, the committee leaders track to the dessert table to collect gobs of what had been two spectacular trifles. The cool whip had melted in the August heat. The meeting reveals only a little of Phyllis's issues. Her speech appears normal.

During the dessert conversation, we are asked to present a slide show at the annual meeting in November. We had prepared the show about the growth of the Austerlitz Historical Society for the Roslyn Landmark Society in February before our trip to Myrtle Beach. Again, we refuse to concede a problem. Regardless of Phyllis's condition, we make commitments to do what we always did. I stuff my angst. It will work out.

One morning 9/11/2001, we are aghast at the plane bombing of the twin towers. I become speechless with Phyllis. Aphasia is not just for the brain impaired. About ten days after the attack, the Spencertown drum corps plays a dolorous drum beat to raise the flag at Autumn in Austerlitz. We keep the day normal, a distraction. About 300 regular attendees show up, thankful for our perseverance. A in A is a success.

The next month we arduously prepare the slide presentation for the AHS meeting. We spend hours looking over the slides and text of the program. We practice the coordination, script to slides. Phyllis can read meaningfully; the show will go on. Reading, conversing, and planning for the presentation becomes therapy.

Dr. Spinner's caution about seizures becomes reality one early autumn evening. While we sit near our toasty wood stove, Phyllis has a slight mouth twitch that becomes major head bobbing. Her eyes, arms and right leg move sporadically. I rush to her side to assure that she is secure in the chair. I embrace her, so she knows I'm there, but I'm helpless to thwart the rage of the seizure. Fifteen minutes pass. I dial 911. A long ten minutes go by before Bryan, the Fire Chief, enters the room. I was his guidance counselor.

"Hey Phil, tell me what's going on." He only wants some basic information. I tell him everything, way more than he needs. "Slow down. The ambulance will be here soon, I just need a few details, and they'll take care of her." The members of the rescue squad are former students from Chatham High. They worked harder at emergency medical treatment than they ever did in their studies. Experienced in emergency care, they dutifully wrap their former teacher in blankets and hoist her onto a stretcher and into the ambulance. I'm dazed as I climb into the front seat and wave to my fellow Austerlitz Volunteer Firemen on traffic control. Despite the care of the emergency team, the reality of a long lonely road haunts me.

The seizures are relentless, continuing the entire way to Columbia Memorial Hospital in Hudson, and as Phyllis is transferred to Albany Medical Center at about 8 p.m. The staff in the ER prepare for the worst. A technician brings in a large wooden box. "It's for intubation," he says and explains that Phyllis seems to be having trouble breathing. That procedure frightens me. It's life support. A little after 10 p.m. the seizures stop, and Phyllis begins to breathe normally. No intubation. About 2 a.m. she opens her eyes and smiles.

"Hi… you're okay!" I say. She doesn't speak, but, acknowledges with her eyes that she is aware. Phyllis is admitted officially to the hospital for evaluation and observation. She insists on doing things on her own, including the short walk to the bathroom. There's the threat of shackles to hold her down at night. Her sister Pat stays with her in the hospital a couple of nights to call the nurse when necessary.

On Sunday, we begin walking. By the nursing station, two or three times per walk. Five walks both Sunday and Monday. We discuss going home and the possibility of chemotherapy with the nurse practitioner, who visits Phyllis on Monday. The NP also conveys a message from Dr. Spinner to raise the Dilantin 50 mg. so it becomes therapeutic. An MRI originally scheduled in two weeks can be done after discharge the next day. No one told us that we would have to wait all day for the MRI chamber to be available. We fidget throughout the day until Phyllis is gurneyed to the MRI in the basement at about 9 p.m. The dimmed evening lights create a surreal eeriness in the shadows. Muted sound. Blue cloaked medical staff moving in the distance. A masked nurse compounds the spectrum as she injects the contrast dye.

"This won't hurt sweetie!" she says as she plunges the needle into Phyllis's vein. More noise, the required resonance, as if from a nearby alley.

The getaway car had been parked near the front door all day. We use a wheelchair to board the elevator. A brief hum, doors slide open on the exit landing. The chair glides down the ramp through the dim parking lot to the car. Phyllis stands. I support her as she pulls herself into the passenger seat. At eleven p.m. we outrun the lights of the city to the refuge of a chilly star-filled night. We're going home, wiser, warier. Anything can happen. Anytime. The next afternoon, we discuss our immediate future, the slide show. "I d-d-don't know if I c-c-can do it, if I can do it," Phyllis manages to say.

"We'll try it out. We'll practice together next week, to see if it will work," I say as I hold her hand, unsure of what will actually happen.

"W-w-what if it d-d-doesn't, it doesn't?" she counters, fully aware that her speaking is problematic.

"I will take care of it, as long as you are there," an attempt to reassure both of us.

A week-long respite from practice helps Phyllis recover a little from her aphasia. We use the week to set up our tall Christmas tree. Phyllis hands me the branches that I press into the main trunk. I put on the lights, the tree's only dress until Thanksgiving. The lights mollify the darkness of the oncoming winter. The lighted tree brightens our spirits.

We go over the script of the slide presentation a few times out loud. Phyllis reads it over, maybe once, on her own when she feels like it.

The third Sunday of November finds us front and center at the old church in Austerlitz before thirty friends, AHS members and non-members. After I introduce the presentation, Phyllis adds, "You'll really like it." Polite applause ushers us to the comfort of our script near the projector. Like an unbalanced stereo, we read our parts, one speaker at high volume, the other, just audible enough. It seems long. Some people turn to me while Phyllis is speaking very softly. I ignore their glance. The fact that we are there presenting is my satisfaction.

Thanksgiving Day follows quickly after the AHS program. The November issue of *Gourmet Magazine* has recipes to please turkey lovers and vegetarians. When Dan, Meg or Pat offer to bring something, I assign them bread, beverages or appetizers. I prepare the turkey and trimmings recipes from *Gourmet* that gives a time table, so all the work doesn't have to be done on the Day. Saturday I shop; Sunday, through Wednesday, I prepare one or two dishes each day: parsnip-apple soup, vegetarian gravy, stuffing, scallions, pumpkin cheesecake. It all comes together

Thanksgiving Day with the roasting of the turkey, and of course the feasting. Phyllis, Pat and Meg fill up on the vegetarian offerings. Dan and I eat the turkey. The cheesecake is delicious. We're happy. I'm exhausted.

I find time to relax while the tree takes on its ornamental coat as everyone helps hang about 400 ornaments. Phyllis passes out song sheets and leads us in *Over the River* with Pat fingering the piano. As we sit around the glistening tree, the discussion turns to the family Christmas party to be held here in ten days. "Can you and Mom do it all?" Meg asks, knowing that her mother may not be up to the task.

"We can get it started, but if you and Dan can help serve, that would be nice," I suggest.

"Whatever you want," Dan offers.

The family Christmas party requires perfection. Phyllis and I clean and dust together, almost always in the same room. We set up tables with forty-five place settings of Christmas china collected over the years, water glasses, and silverware. "Don't forget the mops!" Phyllis advises. She corrects herself. "I mean the mops!", and yet again slightly more irritated, "Don't forget the... mops." Frustrated, she stops, and reaches for a napkin. "You have to put out the mops."

"Oh, okay. The napkins! Boy, that's annoying. Right on the tip of your tongue!" I say as I distribute colorful napkins that she and Pat had hemmed from bright squares of red with green and blue flowers.

Phyllis's idea of a treasure hunt with clues has become a tradition for parties at our house. Items we have collected and wrapped are carefully placed throughout the house. "Knock down the cobwebs as you go," she laughs as she reads the clues. I take each gift to the clued location, armed with a dust cloth.

"The Silent Singer," she reads. I hurry with a treasure to the heirloom treadle sewing machine where I dust and place the gift. "Little Miss Muffet, sat on her tuffet," sends me scurrying to a large cushion in the living room. With "Little Jack Horner, sat in the corner," I skip with the treasure to a dust free corner. When the treasures are out of sight, Phyllis hands me the clues encased in several dozen red stockings to hang on a little tree. The house is clean, dusted in every cranny, and the tables are set. Phyllis sleeps soundly in anticipation of the best Christmas party ever. I toss and turn, elated that we are ready.

The relatives turn out in extra force to show their support. Dan and Meg are all over the place, greeting, taking coats, directing the relatives about the food placement. My sisters provide the lasagna and salad. My brothers provide the wine and beverages. Appetizers, pies and cookies from nieces and nephews overflow on the serving tables. Gifts galore are traded in boxes at the entry door.

Pat leads us in carols and holidays songs. Phyllis divides us into three groups for the *Christmas is coming, the goose is getting fat* round. After the singing, I announce the treasure hunt with a warning that if anyone sees dust, there are rags for them to remove it. The porch drains of people causing a traffic jam around the tiny stocking dressed tree. Fixated on the search, figuring out the clues, no one asks for a dust rag. They avariciously shred the wrappings from their treasures, little candles, toys, and jewelry.

At some point later, I converse with my brother Mike, and his wife Patsy, about the aphasia that Phyllis is experiencing. I mention "the mops." We laugh about its frustrations. Patsy commiserates, "These have been difficult months. You must have cried a lot."

"Yes, it's been difficult," I reply. "But neither Phyllis or I cry much. I don't have time to cry."

This is a time to be bold. I cannot show weakness for Phyllis' sake. I must be strong for Dan and Meg. Minor seizures and speech problems invade our life through the holidays, insignificant interruptions in a flood of fun.

We open our house once more during that holiday time to celebrate a special meal with several of the first people we had met when we came to Austerlitz. Phyllis enjoys having them. They infuse our spirits with lively conversation, laughter, and gratitude. Sometime during all the celebrating, we visit Dr. Spinner. Chemotherapy is on the agenda. "It could be difficult. We can start that after the holidays. Have a Merry Christmas, and I'll see you in January," Spinner says cheerfully as she's about to celebrate with her daughter and infant son.

The usual plethora of gifts under our tree greets our family on Christmas day. It seems Santa knows our house well. A quiet New Year's Eve celebration. Our joint resolution. Laugh more.

16. Treatment Together

Dr. Spinner warned us when we first met her that there is no cure, only treatment. The new year finds us determined to push on with full confidence that we can beat this malady for a several years. My hope is that chemo will halt the tumor forever; maybe reduce it, even to nothingness. Perhaps a cure will be available within a few years, a dream that contributes to my optimism. We do not want the tumor to slow us down. In late January, we are greeted in Spinner's office by the Nurse Practitioner and the news that Dr. Spinner is taking a leave of absence. "Perhaps we shouldn't begin the therapy without her," I suggest.

"We can begin. I have done this before, and one of the other doctors will verify the treatment," the NP says. "It has to happen."

Phyllis's chemotherapy requires her to ingest powerful pills throughout the cycle, ending with a single injection on the third week. The list of side effects on the labels and the warning is frightening: "Report side effects to your doctor. Remember that your doctor has prescribed this medication because he or she has judged that the benefit to you exceeds the risk of side effects."

As the chemo cycle progresses, I have difficulty discerning whether what I witness is a side effect or part of the condition being treated by the chemo. Seizures happen every day. Phyllis has difficulty walking, balancing, and often falls for no reason. By the time I realize these are probably side effects, Phyllis is deep into the cycle. We stagger on with the chemo to complete the horrendous first cycle. My optimism is overwhelmed.

In February, Spinner is back. She notices Phyllis's swollen right foot with a sneaker slit to accommodate it. It's the predicted blood clot. "I can't let you go home like this. The clot has to be treated in the hospital," she says.

Despite the clot, cycle two begins in the hospital. I learn about anticoagulants, the importance of monitoring therapeutic levels of Coumadin, more than I ever wanted to know. The second chemo cycle has none of the side effects of the first cycle.

An MRI reveals no change. Nurse Betty notices I'm not excited about no change. She reminds me that no change is good.

What really confuses me about the "No change" verdict is the change in Phyllis. At some point in early April, I make a list of Phyllis's progress since the onset of chemo. The list reveals how far from normal life has become. I'm happy because Phyllis has "become more active than passive" as evidenced by: *-suggesting a ride or fieldtrip; making an appointment for a manicure; willingness to have visitors; participating in exercise activities; loading and unloading the dishwasher; handling contact lenses; applying makeup; pouring and drinking coffee; getting snacks; email; reading and comprehension; inquiries about the previous 3 or 4 months; taking care of plants and house arrangement. Sleep is better. Incontinence no longer an issue. Still challenged by keyboards, but manages.*

I'm proud of the progress, but when I look over the list again at home, I realize it is a list of things that I was doing most of the year. From entertainment to make-up I had become Phyllis. I comb through *Country Living, Martha Stewart Living,* and *Gourmet Magazine* for ideas about home decor, recipes, makeup and fashion. Togetherness becomes an inextricable oneness. I continue to give her name and birthday when asked at the hospital, the doctor's office, the pharmacy.

Armed with the "No change is good" reassurance from nurse Betty and Spinner, and my own evaluation of the observed improvements, the third cycle begins. The side effects of the first cycle reappear: difficulty walking, occasional falls, frequent seizures. I call the cancer center to report the issues. "Continue with the chemo," is the response. The list of improvements becomes inverted, a list of things Phyllis cannot do again.

On Memorial Day weekend, Phyllis falls and hits her face on the woodwork in the bathroom, despite being accompanied by Meg. Unfortunately, the Coumadin level is beyond therapeutic. I apply an ice pack, as we rush Phyllis to the Albany Med ER. She's treated, observed and released the same day.

Phyllis's engaging blue eyes are blank gray, empty. Her thin porcelain cheek bones are puffy, and dark night blue creeps over her left face. The symmetry is out of whack as the bruise seeps over half of her face in the coming days. Only time and a diminished dose of Coumadin curtails the creeping meandering bruise. On our next visit to Spinner, we agree that the side effects of this chemo are too drastic.

"I want to change the chemo and start some different anti-seizure drugs. You're going to have a summer free from chemo, and maybe from seizures," Spinner says.

We are grateful for the chemo holiday. "We have an important anniversary coming up this summer," I tell Spinner. "It's our thirtieth."

"How will you celebrate it?" Spinner asks.

"I'll be surprised," Phyllis says.

"Happy anniversary! I'll see you in September," Spinner says.

We are married thirty years on June 12. My romantic side screams celebration. My sober self says "Whoa!" Phyllis is unstable. Her face looks awful. Half her face is normal pink and white, and the other half is black and blue, a painful deep contrast. Another fall or seizure can happen any minute.

I'm proud and stubborn, maybe selfish. Courageous or naive; hard to tell. We are going to have some fun celebrating. There's a little picnic area on Lake Mansfield about ten minutes from our house. A lunch, some tea, and cupcakes, relax in the sun for a couple of hours. Restful, a reminder of old times when we escaped to be together before we were married. I pack the car early in the morning despite the rain. Folding chairs, lunch, table cloth, candles, dishes and utensils, and a camera. The rain will stop.

Phyllis takes her shower. I help her wash. I think of the beautiful legs that I knew only a year ago, now heavy and puffy. They still work, but barely. I wonder if she will come back. As I help her dry, I notice her head bobs, once twice. Her mouth appears to have tasted a lemon. She appears dazed. I lead her to the bed where I finish drying her tortured body. The seizure stops. After a short rest, I help her dress. The rain stops. "Let's go," I, the Lord of the Weather, proclaim to my perplexed bride.

Phyllis moves slowly. The effects of the seizure, or just

reluctance to venture into the rain, I'm not sure. I'm fixated on a romance.

"We can do this." I put one arm around her. She takes my other hand for support. We both practically trip down the steps. I had left the car door open, a welcome refuge from the threatening clouds and the flirting sun. At the lake, I again wrap my right arm around Phyllis. She grasps my raincoat for additional support. A tablecloth is tucked under my left arm. We stumble to the closest picnic table where Phyllis settles on a bench while I cart the lunch over.

I fill both cups with iced tea to share the moment. I taste her love and determination. I recall a line from Gibran's poem: *Fill each other's cup but drink not from one cup.* The sandwiches and the cupcakes are perfect for the occasion. Light. Filling enough. Easily consumed.

As Phyllis gazes over the misty lake, the sun no longer visible, I snap her picture. I wonder what she is thinking. Of *thirty years of a wonderful life*. Or *such a miserable day*. Maybe, *he tries so hard to make it fun*. Moments later, I set her up so she can take my picture. There is no one else in the park to snap a picture of the two of us. The photos prove that we celebrated our thirtieth anniversary.

The rain resumes with a fury as we retreat to the car. I feel romantic and foolish. Celebrations are important, but against these odds, I wonder. Thirty years of faithfulness, two wonderful children, successful careers, mostly triumphs, unbridled togetherness. As I drive through the rain, I know another thirty years is impossible. More than five or six. We're going for it.

It is a little over a year since we've returned from Boston. Phyllis has become very dependent on me during the year. I am her support and guide wherever she goes. I maintain the calendar, set up appointments. The relationship has necessarily shifted. As autumn approaches, we decide to go to Cape Cod for a week. Dan and Meg join us for the weekend. The week at the Cape is a week of shopping, hiking the trails, and dining before the new chemo regimen begins.

"How was the anniversary?" Dr. Spinner asks as she enters the room.

"It went well despite rain and seizures. Then we went to the Cape," I said.

"How was that?" Spinner asks, assessing Phyllis's ability to respond.

"It felt normal!" Phyllis exclaims. "Meg came with her dog for a couple of days, and some friends also came."

After the usual neurological tests and the blood work, Phyllis is cleared to take the powerful chemo pills. The pills are ingested only during the first five days of the thirty-day cycle. A return visit to Spinner in four weeks. Twelve cycles in all. A full year. A list of reactions comes with the medications. Seizures are on the list. I don't blame the chemo for seizures.

We deserve another vacation after the first week of chemo, so we drive a few hours to Hampton Beach, N.H., an hour from Meg's home in Boston. It's autumn so I leave the bathing suits home; the ocean is bitter cold here no matter the season. Our condo is a block from the beach, but near the

Kittery, Maine outlet shops, and Strawberry Bank, an historical preservation in Portsmouth, New Hampshire. Despite the chemo, Phyllis, seems strong. Seizures seem to occur regularly at three-month intervals, but are less intense, and shorter in duration. I don't expect to see one on this vacation.

Phyllis tries to do things on her own. The second night at Hampton Beach, I fall asleep quickly. Phyllis doesn't. When I roll over. I notice she's missing. I call softly. She replies, "I'm making hot chocolate, but the microwave doesn't work." I notice her stabbing the start button several times.

"It did earlier for dinner; let me take a look," as I softly touch her hand to remove it from the machine where persistence fails. She's right. The microwave doesn't light up at all. It has shut down from overheating. On the counter rests a cup of totally cold hot chocolate. "You have to put it in the microwave," I joke with a sleepy grin.

"Oh, no wonder it didn't get hot!" she responds.

I laugh as I pour the hot chocolate into a saucepan. I add extra for myself. The trusty stove top never fails. "Why didn't you wake me up?" I ask.

"You have been doing a lot lately; I didn't want to disturb you. Besides, I wanted to do something myself." We sip the hot chocolate. It's cozy and loving until shouts erupt. An angry customer is berating the night manager. The cops come to quell tempers.

"We better wait until morning to tell him about the microwave," Phyllis suggests. In the cool of the night, the

85

microwave cures itself. It cooks our oatmeal in the morning.

As the week goes on, we visit Strawberry Bank twice, march around downtown Portsmouth, shop at the Kittery Outlets, where we purchase a wreath and Nutcracker ornaments for our tree. We walk the windy boardwalk and beach. Meg visits us for a day at Strawberry Bank, and we travel to see her in Boston on another day. Phyllis directs me to pull into Dunkin Donuts daily and sometimes more than daily, to purchase a half dozen glazed. It reminds me of her occasional repetitive speech. The frequent stops are ultimate delicious perseveration.

17. We have parties

The holidays of 2002 resemble the previous year. The tree is up in mid-November and trimmed on Thanksgiving Day by our dinner guests. The extended family of about fifty comes for the annual Christmas party, the second weekend after Thanksgiving. In the holiday spirit, Phyllis suggests that we invite the neighbors in for a party. "I would like to thank them for their support throughout the year. They have visited, called and sent food."

"Okay. I'll make some invitations. Let's figure out whom to invite." The list is narrowed to twenty-five. We set December 21st, the winter solstice, as the date for our holiday supper. Twenty-four neighbors indicate they will come. Four large tables and twenty-four chairs crowd around the splendid tree on the porch. Christmas china surrounds the candles in the center of each table. We hurriedly shop for additional flatware. Plastic is not an option. To preserve an element of surprise, Phyllis wants the door to the porch closed when our guests arrive. I post a sign on the locked porch door with Phyllis's wording: "Pub will open at 6:45. Appetizers and drinks are served in the kitchen until then."

For my own sanity, I post on the fridge a schedule of last-minute duties. *5:00- put out salads; 5:45- turn on the oven, fill the water glasses; 6- put the lasagna in the oven; plug coffee urn in when the lasagna is done.* Pre-heating the oven and pressing the button for the coffee are crucial. Failure in either area will cause problems. Treasures peek out from all over anxious to be discovered by the guests. "This is exciting," I say gleefully rubbing my hands.

"Wait till they see that tree!" Phyllis says, exuding pride after all the preparation. We relax and revel for only a short time. The unexpected happens about four in the afternoon. After three months without a seizure, Phyllis's brain decides it is time. She knows what's happening. I help her to bed. It doesn't stop quickly. I call the neighbors. They are upset and concerned. I assure them, "All is well. We will re-schedule." I try to be confident as the seizure continues for an hour or more. It's difficult to tell whether it is one continuous seizure or a series of smaller ones. Head bobbing and mouth sucking, biting on the right cheek, right eye blinking uncontrollably. When the seizure relents, during a period of calm, I tell Phyllis about the cancellation. She's disappointed but relieved. After I put away all the perishable food, I turn out the lights. We'll get back to this, I think. Phyllis sleeps restlessly, interrupted with occasional seizure activity. I sleep even less being interrupted by seizures and thinking about the wisdom of a party this year. Maybe it still can work.

The next morning, Phyllis walks with me to the porch. Testimony to the party that had not happened permeates the house. The small tree decorated with the red stockings that holds the clues to treasures, some hidden in plain sight. The array of wine glasses for two dozen people. The quiet piano with a stack of song sheets. The tables set up and ready for food and conversation have designated places for each guest. "Change this ...," Phyllis says. She moves her name card to the place next to mine, sending someone to another table. "I want to sit. Just... will we have the?"

The party is not going away. In three days, it's Christmas. "We'll have to wait until after Christmas," I say.

88

"Oh," is her frustrated reply. It's a big deal for her.

"We'll leave things in place," I suggest. She wants to wander and stumble.

"The coffee is ready. It was set up last night. I just pressed the button as we walked by." I escort her to the den and serve coffee and Panettone there.

"How do you feel now?"

"I was excited about the party," she replies. "Can we have it after Christmas? Will people come?"

"They'll come whenever we decide to have it. There isn't much going on around here."

"We're it!" Phyllis says. Some steadiness has returned to her demeanor.

"We'll enjoy our kids for Christmas and then get back to the party," I promise as I slice the Panettone

Phyllis rests in her chair. Weary and alone, I return to the porch to get ready for Christmas day. I stack some dishes, consolidate the glasses and napkins, push some tables and chairs aside. Later in the day, I invite Phyllis to view my rearrangement. She smiles when I announce, "Santa has room for the gifts."

On Christmas day, Santa fills all the vacant space with presents. Meg's boxer, Zeus, in his terrible twos joins Pat, Meg,

Dan, Phyllis, and me around the tree on a snowy Christmas morning. He enjoys a romp over, around and among the gifts. Zeus finds a bone, his new bed, and contentment. We tear off wrapping paper to find warm and enjoyable treasures. Candy laden stockings droop by the fireplace, each garnished with a large peppermint cane. Mixed nuts trickle onto the floor as we search the stockings for the gifts too small to go under the tree; gift cards to Macy's, Walmart, the Olive Garden; colorful fragrant soaps; an egg separator; and a large navel orange in the toe.

Brunch follows with tomato mushroom omelet accompanied by an array of quick breads: cranberry nut, banana nut, zucchini nut and a torte.

The snow continues throughout the day. I'm anxious. There's enough caring company in the house. I don my new knit hat and gloves for a long walk with my camera. Traffic is absent along route 22. Visibility is zero. Audibility? I scream the unutterable sounds, my sadness, my frustration that has been bouncing in my brain, tearing at my heart. A quarter mile of obscenities, months of tension, blowing away in the blizzard of '02.

The snow draped Old Austerlitz Village viewed through the snowflakes comprises a beautiful photo. As I trudge home, I admire the fury of the storm, the wind stretching out the American flag at the firehouse, the spray of snow coming from the North, and the silence imposed as life in the valley comes to a halt. A waft of smoke from our house's chimneys tells me that Dan tends the fires in the stoves and the fireplace. Warmth welcomes me as I hug Phyllis dozing in her chair. Joy will win.

The day after Christmas, at Meg's suggestion, I go for

another walk before she returns to Boston. Only plows seem to be out on the snow packed road. Again, I'm the only person. With no one to listen, I sing "Good King Wenceslaus," a song about the King of Bohemia who walked through the snow to take care of the poor on the day after Christmas. I again photograph snow stacked Old Austerlitz Village gleaming in the sun. I return up the highway feeling grateful for some good times. I shovel off Meg's car singing "Let it Snow" and help pack her presents in the trunk and front seat, so Zeus can stretch out in the back.

"When do the neighbors come?" Meg asks.

"S-s-soon." Phyllis responds.

"Need any help?" Dan offers.

"We're all set. Maybe you can help move the tables back." Both Dan and Meg arrange the tables for the party. When the road is cleared, and the driveway plowed, both Dan and Meg drive away.

As soon as they leave, Phyllis turns to me and with a soft hug says, "How about New Year's Eve?"

I test the waters with a call to Bob Herron. Bob had become a close friend over the years. His general knowledge, instant humor and insight brighten our house. He's an Austerlitz treasure. We consider him necessary to a happy party. "I figured you'd call. How's Phyllis?" he says.

"She's doing well; we're trying to figure out when to have the party. I'm calling you first," I say as I smile towards Phyllis. She appears excited that Bob will accept my suggestion.

"You're still going to have it?" he asks.

"Yes. The tables are set. What do you think of New Year's Eve?"

"Well that might not be good," he asserts. "People have things going on; I know I do."

"Okay! You answered my question. We can aim for next week. Maybe Wednesday?" I suggest.

"Any day is good that week," he assures me

"Put Wednesday on your calendar. I'll get back to you," I tell him. "See you then."

He repeats "See you!"

I turn to Phyllis. "That was short. We'll have the party next Wednesday. He has something going on New Year's Eve, and he thinks others do too."

She smiles, "Y, y, y, yes!"

On New Year's Eve day, thanks to CNN, we watch every celebration throughout the world, fireworks galore: Sydney, Singapore, Athens, and more. In the evening, we drink a quiet toast and watch the Times Square celebration. We resolve again to laugh more.

At about 5 p.m. the following Wednesday, Phyllis and I

place a handful of salad greens on the salad plates. A little later, she drops a few ice cubes in each water glass. I follow her with a pitcher of water. It looks peaceful. But dim with only an overhead light. The room is ready. I check salads and water off the to-do list.

Shortly after 6 p.m., the dessert table overflows with kuchen, pineapple upside down cake, cheesecake, cookies and pastries. The appetizer table teases with deviled eggs, assorted cheeses, crackers. Sour cream dip surrounded with fresh vegetables. We have locked the porch where dinner is to be served. Only Phyllis and I know what's behind the door.

Guests have uncertain expectations after the postponement. They try to avoid curious questions about Phyllis's condition. I whisper to them, "She's fine." When they see her interacting and smiling, conversation becomes normal. Over wine, beer, and flavored seltzer water, we taste, laugh, and hug. About 6:45, I sneak onto the porch, turn on the tree lights, and light the candles on the tables. I peek over my shoulder. *What a sight!*

Ting a ling! Ting! Ting! Phyllis stands near the piano and presses a little bell that adorned her desk in her classroom a few years ago. The guests quiet in attention. I welcome them. "We thank you for coming on such short notice, and we thank you for your support over the past year. There are place cards at the tables, so everyone is mixed up. Relax and enjoy supper." The door swings open. One by one they file into the room. The tree dazzles them. "Wow!" "Just like the Nutcracker!" "How did you get that tree in here?"

I direct some guests to their seats rather than have them wandering around. Phyllis and I sit down last. She leans toward me, "This is perfect!" Phyllis pushes her salad greens around. I barely touch mine. I notice when people are finished. Guests help clear the tables and bring in the lasagna. Lasagna is comfort. Lasagna is happy. Lasagna is magic.

Quiet, comfortable conversation ensues. The guests help each other to seconds, and then help clear the tables. I announce, "Coffee and cups are in the kitchen, desserts are on the kitchen table."

"Don't for- for-g-g-get the treasure hunt," Phyllis reminds me.

"Yes, right… before you have coffee and dessert, go into the living room. There is a small tree with red stockings, enough for everybody. Inside the stockings there is a piece of paper with a clue on it. Follow the clue to your treasure."

"Where are they hidden?" someone shouts.

"Mostly in the living room and kitchen areas," I respond. The porch empties in seconds as the neighbors, mostly in their seventies, rush like school children, to find a trophy. Bob Herron speaks confidentially to me. "I know there is a Singer sewing machine somewhere, but I can't remember where it is."

"Ha! Okay, just turn around and look behind the blue chair." He's off.

Another says to me. "I know my treasure is in the potato bin, but where is that?" I direct him to the kitchen. The treasures represent a supply of re-gifts, soaps, kitchen tools, fans and other oddities. We have cleaned house.

Coffee and dessert lead into our holiday sing-a-long. When Pat warms up on the piano, the song sheets distribute themselves. *Carolina in the mornin', Take me out to the ball game, "Silent Night"* one after another, twelve songs. Cheer is palpable. We confront 2003 with an abundance of love and confidence.

Something good is happening. Chemo continues, and a degree of normalcy returns to life. Two years ago, at Denny's, we decided to continue to have fun, travel and party. Our first efforts have been rewarding in a mixed-up way. Seizures, treatments, medications are dangerous rocks in a meandering stream. Although it is treacherous, the river is full of life. We learn to navigate.

We celebrate with annual parties for the neighbors and the family at Christmas time. We fete birthdays and Thanksgiving. We attend weddings and funerals.

At our niece's wedding, September 2006.

18. On the Road

We travel to Williamsburg, Virginia and the Long Island Sound in Connecticut.

After the neighbors' party, we become housebound, venturing out to see the doctor or to shop. We are hopeful that chemo will keep the tumor at bay. A seizure happens sometime in February. It's short, maybe ten minutes. I realize that there's a good chance that another seizure will not occur for three months. Perhaps in May. Time for a vacation.

I rent a studio apartment at Patriot's Place in Williamsburg for a week near the end of March. After an overnight in northern Maryland, we arrive at the apartment in the late afternoon in the pouring rain.

The studio is on the second floor. Neither first floor units nor elevators are available. The five steps up to the porch are manageable. We both move fast. I hold an umbrella over Phyllis. She doesn't say much as we enter the hallway. Then she gazes up at what must appear to her to be an endless staircase. "Are you crazy?" she says.

"One step at a time!" I reply feeling as if I am crazy.

She gamely tackles the stairs, quietly making her way to the top. A few more steps to the room. "By the end of the week, I'll be better at this," she quips as she kicks off her wet shoes and sprawls onto the bed.

"You're such a good sport to put up with me the way you do!" I exclaim as I fall into bed beside her, exhausted from the drive, and the tension of our lives.

"Let's just have fun!" she consoles me as she dozes off. On tiptoe I depart into the rain to unload the car.

The studio has a mini-kitchen. I heat up a macaroni and cheese casserole that I had made before we began our trip. Throughout the week, I prepare light evening meals here. We enjoy lunch at the historic site most days.

The Williamsburg Historic site is five minutes away. In our optimism about life, we purchase tickets that allow us to return to the site as often as we want that week and over the next year. Every day during that week we choose a destination in the Historic area. Bassett Hall, the former home of John D. Rockefeller, a driving force behind the Williamsburg preservation, is open for the first time ever. The bus line from the Visitors' Center stops near there. It's easy for Phyllis to tour the house and walk the grounds. The tour is mostly on the first floor. Among the manicured lawns, trimmed hedges, neat rows of sprouting herbs and lettuce, random clusters of crocuses struggle through rotted leaves. I read her mind and say to Phyllis, "We can do the crocuses."

Phyllis has had her tour for the day. The handicapped accessible bus arrives and bows down to ground level for Phyllis to walk in. After a quick survey of the gift shops at the Visitors' Center, we head for our studio. Phyllis mounts the stairs, quietly, and again collapses on the bed, tired, happy, in a place she loves.

The next day, with the ill effects of the last dose of chemo fading, we return to the Historic Site with renewed energy. The bus leaves us a couple blocks from the Raleigh Tavern. After a gentle stroll down the street, where horse drawn carriages ferry well-heeled visitors, we arrive at the Tavern. A troupe of performers in colonial costume regale us with tales as they lead us through the downstairs rooms. Phyllis's energy wanes. The bartender notices, and invites us to rest in the comfort of the taproom. As we sit close together at small table, a gaily dressed gentleman in a fine but shabby suit, and a wig, appears near the table. "May I join your company?"

"Have a seat," I say reaching to slide out an empty chair.

"You are not from around here, I can tell," he says.

"No, we're from New York," I reply.

"A magnificent city, I'm told," he says maintaining his period demeanor.

We time travel to 1776 as we talk. If we refer to back then, he says "back when?"

"We live a full day's ride north of the city," I say. "A town called Upper Green River, in the mountains near Massachusetts."

"You're friends with the Adamses, I suppose" he says revealing his ignorance of the geography of Massachusetts.

"They live near Boston, the other end of the Commonwealth. What's your story?" I ask.

"I'm one of many Dance Masters who work in and around Williamsburg. Dance is an entertainment available for both gentlemen and ladies together. An opportunity to meet and greet. A way for the men to show their stuff, and their taste, by the women whom they choose as partners. Many a politician wins or loses because of his dancing ability and the partner who accompanies him," he tells us. He invites us to a lesson that afternoon at his studio across the street. "You are most welcome, and I do hope you participate."

We assure him that we will take dancing lessons that afternoon. When the tour descends the stairs, we overhear conversations about the living conditions in the Tavern. Our conversation with the pleasant Dance Master, about his efforts to raise the level of civility in the colony of Virginia, seems much more interesting. After a light lunch across the street at Shield's Tavern, Phyllis says "I think the Dance Master is waiting for us."

We hustle to the studio a couple doors away. About a dozen people fit into the little room. "Ready to dance?" the Dance Master inquires. "Who wants to perform?"

"Should I do this?" I whisper to Phyllis.

She smiles, squeezes my hand, "You don't need to make a fool of yourself here. Someone will volunteer."

I fidget a bit, and an unabashed party of six are more than willing to be the guinea pigs for the country dance. The Dance Master demonstrates the simple steps, high on his toes, light on his feet, pirouetting and strutting through the lesson. When the volunteer students take to the floor, I'm happy Phyllis holds my hand so tightly. The dancers turn left or right, move in a circle or

100

not, tromping rather than dancing. I had imagined the precision of a clock mechanism. I see six random bouncing balls, rarely in sync. They enjoy the chaos. The Dance Master doesn't mind. Sociability is paramount. Many more lessons are needed before this group is ready for the ballrooms of Colonial Williamsburg. The Dance Master will earn his keep. My elegant lady Phyllis elevates me above the crowd.

And so it goes for the week at Williamsburg, one attraction a day. Phyllis with increased strength and stamina daily. The climb up to the studio becomes less and less of a chore. A good week, and our tickets expire next year.

The Williamsburg trip whets our appetite to venture out again in late spring. Just as winter seemed to hang on too long, spring also hangs on.

In late April, Dr. Spinner is concerned that Phyllis is losing weight very quickly. Spinner suspects one of the anti-convulsants to be the cause and changes the dosage to taper it off to nothing. Despite my anxiety about taking away an anti-convulsant, three good things happen. The anorexia is stymied. Phyllis becomes more alert. The absence of the medication did not promote seizures.

On the prowl for spring, we head to the Connecticut shore for a week at Waters' Edge Resort. When a valet offers to unload the car, I object until I realize the distance from the parking lot to our door is about fifty feet. I let him load the two suitcases, cooler, and a of couple other bags onto a dolly, which he drags across the rain puddled lot to our condo.

To my dismay, our suite is on the second floor. "I should have checked on this when I made the reservation," I apologize to Phyllis as I shake my head in disbelief.

"It's okay: I can do it," Phyllis assures me. "I've had practice." She squeezes my hand with confidence. "I want to give him the tip."

I hand Phyllis five dollars. The bill crumbled in her left hand between her pinky and palm. Her right hand firmly grasps the railing. She reaches across with her left hand to gain extra leverage with her free fingers and thumb. Pull, up with the left foot, right foot rests; pull, left foot rises, right foot rests; fourteen steps. Determined to climb this mountain, total focus. Indomitably inching up the stairs, resolute to place the bill into the valet's hands. I hover close in the scent of her Jean Nate´. I fear a collapse, so I watch that her feet go high enough. I relish the triumph as she conquers each next step. I get an ethereal rush as Phyllis stretches her arm with the crinkled five dollars, concluding the pilgrimage on her knees on the top step before the patient, obliging valet. He steadies her. Phyllis thanks him as she kneels in adoration.

The valet lifts Phyllis to her feet and to the landing; he swiftly relieves her of the five dollars, and escorts her into the room, where she immediately finds the bedroom. While she sprawls on the huge bed, I unpack the luggage and boxes.

As at Williamsburg, she increases in strength as the days pass, able to scale those stairs two or three times a day. After a week that includes daily brunch at the resort, two trips each to Mystic Seaport and the factory outlets, several walks along the shore, the weight loss is reversed. Later in the week the valet remarks "Your wife seems much better."

Yes!

Since Phyllis began to read *Constantine's Sword*, it isn't long before we rejoin the book discussion group. Everyone is supportive. When Phyllis says the opposite of what she means, they repeat what they understand.

"I think you are saying." "You said the opposite of what I think you mean."

"At least I'm thinking. That's good," she says with a self-deprecating laugh.

Most of what has been discussed in the group was an exercise in taking apart our time-honored beliefs. I thought this needed to be done. I also thought that we should take time to write down what we believe now. I suggest that we write summaries of what we currently believe and read these to the group. I forget the challenge that this presents to Phyllis, and promise to help her with the assignment. We invite the group to our house for the next meeting. I write my diatribe. Too much anger and toss it away. I write something related to my life, emphasizing the importance of personal responsibility in dealing with life's problems. This is a value that had been impressed on me by my parents. It speaks to my current situation as I promote a wholesome life for Phyllis and the family.

Phyllis is more creative. She knows her limitations. She bakes gingerbread cookies for everyone. With amusement, I help her measure the flour and combine the ingredients. She cuts a few of the figures enough for everyone plus a few extras. She decorates most of them with tiny red cinnamon for eyes, nose and mouth. I do the remaining few. I put them in the oven and onto a cooling rack when done. Together we wrap the individual cookies and tie a bow on each. With that task completed, I wonder what Phyllis's next step is. We share one of the extras for dessert.

In the morning of the day the discussion group is to meet at our house, Phyllis sits thoughtfully in her chair. Pen in hand. I don't notice much writing, but after a half of an hour, she puts the pen aside. "Finished!" she says as she hands the paper to me. "Make enough copies for everyone." I glance at it quickly and give her a big hug.

"You did it without my help. Wow!" I exclaim still hugging her.

Phyllis is excited as the group participants assemble. Most have traveled from Albany.

We go around the room with each person reading a two-page statement outlining their personal beliefs after several years of study with the group. We seem to be on the same page of life. Phyllis stands up and brings a small tray with an array of gingerbread men and women. She distributes on cookie to each person. I think the people appreciate the break after the somewhat weighty thoughts that had been expressed.

Phyllis has their attention and takes out her stack of papers. She reads to the hushed expectant group, "I cannot talk, but I can love. God is love. Phyllis."

By my reckoning, it's been a pretty good year. Travel, parties and return to the discussion group. Being with each other. Chemo is having a positive effect. Phyllis seems to be coming back. That list of things she can do is positive again. Chemo will end in October after a full year of monthly doses of Temodar.

19. Detours Along the Way

No one other than Dan, Meg and Phyllis's sister Pat has yet witnessed the writhing insanity that accompanies the seizures that Phyllis experiences. We manage to deal with them by viewing them as normal. A part of life that we try to anticipate and control as much as possible. I approximate them at three-month intervals. Sometimes, one occurs a week or two beyond three months. Other times, it is a few days shorter. Around these times, we stay close to home, the most comfortable place for the inevitable.

Long range commitments throw a monkey wrench into my predictive ability. On an August day, I'm the officiant at the wedding of a neighbor who's marrying his high school sweetheart. I have the privilege of performing weddings because I was an elected Town Justice for Austerlitz justice in the early 1980s. The privilege endures all these years.

I remember that it has been about three months since the last seizure, and I'm hoping that today is not the day. Any notion of a seizure occurring fades into the background in the face of this beautiful wedding at the Mount Lebanon Shaker Village in Lebanon Springs, New York. Two families are joined in the glow of candles, amorous poetry, simple harp music, vows and declarations. Phyllis is happy to be seen and to participate in the life of these young people whom she has taught and loved. We sit near the front of the large meeting room, where I can be the official witness for the State of New York, declare them husband and wife, and introduce the new Mr. and Mrs.

Immediately after the ceremony, the wedding party disappears for photographs. Phyllis and I sneak away from the crowd to admire a trail of Shaker artifacts, the panoramic view from the Mount, and spectacular early evening sky. We are in tune with the peaceful place and the people who inhabited it many years ago. When we return to enjoy a cocktail with old friends, brief conversations simulate a debut for Phyllis with people whom she hasn't seen in years. They had heard stories about her medical condition and are surprised to see her feeling so well. It begins to get chilly as the sun sets. A slight breeze causes us to retreat to the banquet tent that has canvas sides to ward off the evening coolness. While the bride and groom appear at the cocktail reception, Phyllis and I bundle up in the banquet tent a hundred yards away. Our teeth chatter. I notice an ominous twitch near Phyllis's right lip. She's not talking.

"We better sit down!" I urge as I usher her a few yards to a seat at our designated table. While cocktails flow in the reception tent, I hold her close to warm her, hoping the twitch will remain only slight. Ten minutes later, the guests come into the tent to find me clutching Phyllis, trying to keep her from falling off her metal folding chair. Probably she would have been better off on the ground, but I had several reasons why that shouldn't happen. Her dress would be a mess. It would be an ugly sight. When she might be able to move, it would be difficult to get her off the ground.

The guests do not know exactly what is happening. There are offers to help. The flimsy chair is being driven into the ground as Phyllis forcefully rocks and sways. The seat is a little more than a foot above the grass, partially bent in several places.

What could be an easily managed home situation becomes an "emergency" in the minds of the wedding guests. "No, don't call the rescue squad," I yell to a person who offers to

108

call. I'm concerned that such a call would hospitalize Phyllis for no reason other than observation. Besides, I want to avoid the hysteria that accompanies the appearance of emergency services at any event. I can handle this without the medics.

Dan and Meg are the help I need. "What can we do?" Meg asks squatting by her mother's side.

"I am trying to keep Mom from falling." Meg pulls up a chair and sits on the other side.

I tear my car keys from my pocket. Dan grabs them. I didn't know Dan could run so fast. In no time, he has the car parked outside the nearest tent opening. The seizure abates somewhat. Meg and I help Phyllis to stand and guide her to the car. Phyllis somehow helps herself into the car. I fasten her seat belt. I'm ready to go when the paperwork that must be signed by the witnesses appears from nowhere. The witnesses come to the car, startled by the scene, but manage to sign where I tell them. I tuck the license into my pocket so I can make the marriage official when I mail it to the Town Clerk.

"Do you want us to come?" Meg asks.

"No. Stay here, enjoy the party. We'll be okay," I assure her with a hug.

The seizure activity continues off and on for the thirty-minute ride home. Phyllis staggers into the house with my support and into the bedroom where she lies down. It's nearly 10 p.m. "Do you want some Ativan? It may help you relax," I suggest.

109

"If I take that, we can't go back to the party," she responds.

"I don't think we should go back. You need some rest," I say as I brush back some hair that has fallen into her eyes. I see a blank stare. I know she's disappointed. "Then I'll take the Ativan." The party is over for us. I help her change into her nightie. The Ativan induces sleep.

The next day, in the mid-morning sunshine, Phyllis seems reflective about the beautiful wedding. When Dan and Meg stop in for a visit, she asks them about it. "A lot of people were upset," Meg says.

Phyllis seems perplexed as to how to respond. I express her thoughts. "I know. The seizure became a big deal. I guess it had to happen sometime." I choke on my words.

"They seemed to have fun anyway," Dan assures me with a pat on my back.

Despite my calm at the wedding, I had been traumatized by the whole incident. Meg and Dan provided tremendous support when they witnessed their mother's distress. Moments like these prepare us for the shocks that we know will still come. We reflect on this. We remember the grand occasion of two young people joined in love for better or worse.

For better or worse, in sickness and in health. I remember our wedding over thirty years ago. It was much simpler in every way. Once we decided it was time to get married, we set a date. We conferred with a John Kirwin who would perform the ceremony, and less than a week later, we met him again on a

110

Monday night. My father and mother, siblings and spouses, my nephews and nieces, eighteen in all, plus two of Phyllis's friends from the convent, came. My brother George was the best man, and Phyllis's sister Pat was the maid of honor.

When we arrived at the Newman Center, we were the first people there. We escorted each other arm in arm into the parlor for the ceremony. Phyllis turned on a tape of Mozart. My sister Mary appeared armed with pins and boutonnieres for my father, brother George and me. Kirwin arrived next, followed by most of my family and Phyllis's friends.

"You really want to do this?" Kirwin asked in his big voice.

"We're ready," we say simultaneously.

Mozart continues to play in the background as John begins. "I'm here to witness your wedding vows. You do the marrying," he proclaims.

I go first, reciting my vow. "I love you Phyllis and I want you to be my wife. I take you now as my wife. I will love, honor and cherish you for as long as we live. Your life is my life, your spirit is my spirit. We are one." No hesitation. No nervous sweat. Just a true sound of a voice determined and free, giving myself to another human being. My thoughts, derived from years of study and teaching, from officiating as others came to the altar, poured out with certainty, sincerity and finality far different from the meek "Promitto" that I mumbled on ordination day six years and two weeks before.

Phyllis responded, "Philip, you are the world to me. I love you and will spend the rest of my days with you as my husband. We are one and you alone fulfill my heart's desire, for as long as we live." The unscripted words welled up from deep within, the sum of our many conversations about love, choices, and unity. No resemblance to the medieval play-acting years before on the day of her final vows. We realized that we had accomplished the impossible.

John proclaimed us husband and wife. My mother cheered. Others wept in the joy of the moment. The first official kiss, passionate, public, evoked shouts and applause. While George and Pat signed the marriage license, Phyllis and I glowed as we held each other in a relaxed embrace without embarrassment. It was all okay. A simple reception was held at my sister Jean's house, where we drank a champagne toast and gently fed each other pieces from the two-tiered cake baked and decorated by my mother.

When we left the reception after an hour for our honeymoon at Indian Lake in the Adirondacks, my brother Mike, and Jean's husband Bill, had playfully tied tin cans to our car bumper to announce the joy of the newlyweds. The wedding served us well through the years. In these difficult times, we enjoy life.

***

In early September, a month after the wedding, Phyllis and I visit Dr. Spinner. Phyllis's blood work, strength, and awareness are all good. The fact that the seizure at the wedding was shorter than others is encouraging. The year of monthly doses of oral chemotherapy seem to have produced results.

112

Although there is no change in the tumor, there has been a vast change in Phyllis. The chemo treatment seemed gentle compared to the shuffling broken bodies that I had witnessed in the waiting room, who hooked up to an IV for long injections of chemo. We were fortunate to avoid, that as we dealt with the seizures, aphasia and blood clots. "Thanks for being gentle with the chemo," I say to Spinner.

"This was not gentle. It is powerful therapy. Phyllis tolerated it well," Spinner reminds me. I'm chastised and grateful.

"I would like Phyllis to have a gallium scan," Spinner says. "It's at Nuclear Medicine on the sixth floor. It will give us a benchmark. We can monitor any changes if any cancerous tissue develops."

Phyllis is leery of this process. "This isn't radiation?"

"No, just a scan so we know what's going on. It's open, no tube. The machine rotates around your head. No noise."

"Can Phil be in the room?" Phyllis asks, reaching for my hand.

"Yes! He can," Spinner responds. The appointment is set for early December.

With a degree of stability, shorter seizures, and the dissolution of the blood clots, I believe we have exited a dark tunnel. We are riding a wave of energy. We approach Thanksgiving with bright lights on our tall tree, ready for the trimming. Dan, Meg and Pat help us welcome my father in his ninety-third year, and my sister Jean and her family. Meg's dog,

113

Zeus, joins us. He cleans the floor. Phyllis is the hostess, assisting with the food preparation, and table setting. She determines the tablecloth, sets out the white napkins, and arranges the place cards.

A green bean casserole, mashed potatoes, cabbage salad, deviled eggs, cheese and crackers and pies, both apple and pumpkin, all arrive with the guests on Thanksgiving Day. Meg fills a Hubbard squash with beans and rice, an eye-catching vegetarian entree that rivals the roast turkey for attention. After the meal, the guests place the hundreds of ornaments on the lighted tree. The reflective ornaments, combined with the lights produce a whimsical corona. "It feels like old times," Phyllis says as we all rest in the glow of the magnificent tree, sated with food, drink and laughter.

The next week, we attend the eightieth birthday of a close friend. While I learn about his service as a dentist in the army during World War II, Phyllis is engaged in a conversation with another guest whom she had not met before. From what I hear of that conversation, it deals with their common interest in literature. Later in the evening, the hostess mentions to the guest, "Phyllis seems to be doing well. That chemo seems to have done something to the brain tumor."

"Impossible!" the guest exclaims. "She couldn't have a brain tumor."

On the way home, we talk of recovery. "Maybe we are getting back to normal," Phyllis says.

"Yes," I agree. "It has been a long haul."

114

The next day, we travel to Albany Med for the gallium scan. It's in a different part of the hospital from what we're used to, a floor dedicated to nuclear medicine. A view from the window reveals the coned cooling tower. The nuclear age has mixed blessings. There is no comfort in that view despite the benefits.

"Nuclear Medicine Laura" greets us in the waiting room. That's how she answers the phone. "Good afternoon. Nuclear medicine. Laura. Please hold." Dozens of times an hour she repeats these words as she juggles patients' confidential business at the counter. She has us fill out papers, and then we wait.

The waiting room is tiny. Nothing is private. I don't want to talk. "I wish we had some paper," I say to Phyllis. She hands me a brochure with a blank page. After scribbling a few seconds with a Bic pen that I found on a nearby table, I write: *"Dear..."*

I hand Phyllis the pen. She writes: *"Dad, I'm here to get a gallium scan."*

"Why?" I write. We write back and forth.

"I don't know." "What can I tell you about it?"

"They want to know if there is any cancer-- I think. " "That's correct."

"I wish that I would stop coughing." "It will stop for the Christmas party."

"I'm happen to do the Christmas party. But there is much to do."
"I thought we were almost done."

"That girl in charge only has one ear to work with." *"She does everything."*

Phyllis notices that the page is filled. She gets up confidently and asks Nuclear Laura for a sheet of paper, and returns with paper in hand. We continue our antiphonal writing. *"Great! For a minute, I thought she was going to say 'No,'"*

"She was looking for a sheet that didn't have any information on it. I think that those people must think I am deaf and dumb." *"No way!"*

Phyllis glances at a sign pinned to the counter. Then writes, *"Whew! Did you notice I can refuse radioactive stuff?"* *"Yes, but this is not radiation. You can refuse anything you want."*

"Good!" I notice another sign. *"How about the confidentiality sign? Can you imagine discussing anything confidentially here?"*

Phyllis writes, *"No way! Are you hungry?"* *"Yes, I can't wait for lunch. What shall we serve the neighbors this year?"* I write.

"I don't know. Shall we find out who's coming?" *"Okay."*

"Bob?" she writes. Bob Herron is our number one neighbor and guest.

When a nurse interrupts our scrawling conversation, I'm happy that the procedure will begin. I wish I had more time for this conversation. Phyllis is engaged in so many ways. I'm sure there's no cancer, and the tumor has been beaten.

116

The nurse injects the gallium isotope into Phyllis's arm. After a short wait while the isotope circulates, the hour-long scan begins. A nuclear device circles Phyllis's head hunting for cancerous cells luminescent with the isotope. "The scan is negative," the nurse reports over her shoulder, as she releases Phyllis from the table after the scan.

With the preliminary assessment that cancer is not an issue, we head to *Grandma's* restaurant for lunch. Phyllis orders baked macaroni and cheese. I opt for liver and onions. We both have *Grandma's* apple pie for dessert. We take one pie to go, to share with the family at the Christmas party.

On the following cold December Saturday, the wood stoves blaze a warm welcome. On the party day a bounty of fine food, raucous joyful songs, and gifts mixed with snow flurries, envelop forty-five family members, my Dad, my siblings, their spouses, children and their grandchildren.

On Christmas eve and day, Pat joins Meg and Dan as celebrate a quiet Christmas with a huge gift swap, including gifts from Santa.

Finally, before the New Year begins, we invite the neighbors for supper at our house. Appetizers, olives, cheese and crackers, veggies and dips from half of the neighbors quickly fill one table. The other half bring Kuchen, pineapple upside down cake and dozens of cookies for the dessert table. Candle-lit windows, the dazzling tree, and the aroma of carrot soup. Nirvana.

Nothing interferes with the celebration. Pat plays the old piano, "Take me out to the Ball Game," "East Side West Side," and "Silent Night." Voices, great and small, some off key, blend in song and laughter.

The treasure hunt this year reveals Christmas crackers. Tiny festive wrapped tubes filled with more surprises. Everyone finds a partner to pull the tabs at the ends of the crackers to make them crack. Each dons the paper crowns, shares the riddle on the tiny piece of paper, and figures out the unique mini-toys, all found inside the cracker. Crackers are miniature fountains of youth. Everyone is suddenly a child, same ability, same high level of joviality. When the first guests begin looking for their boots to leave, Phyllis rings her teacher bell. "Let's sing to the new year." Those in the room join her as she begins "Should Auld Acquaintance be Forgot." One after another the neighbors depart into the star-studded chilly night, content, happy for this celebration of life.

I have a brief conversation with Wendy Diskin, a special education teacher, who worked closely with Phyllis on the senior program. Wendy provided support for the special needs students who were mainstreamed into Phyllis's classes. "No child left behind" had been enshrined into the law since 2002, requiring more from both students and teachers. More testing which required more preparation for tests. More frustration. "My kids struggle with the new testing requirements. We really miss Phyllis," Wendy quickly replies.

"Maybe I can dig out some of Phyllis's stuff," I suggest.

"That would be so wonderful," Wendy says, as she pulls on her scarf and walks into the night.

20. A Book

I wander into our garage one sunny January afternoon, looking for maps to plan a different route to Williamsburg. I step over and around rakes, shovels, and mowers; piles of spent Christmas wrapping; half empty boxes containing a tool, or stored household item, such as a picture frame or a lamp. I didn't take time to store the tools properly. I didn't have time to take the papers to the dump. I didn't know what to do with the stuff.

The three plastic boxes containing personal papers and memories from our school careers distract me. They had become clutter. I forget about the maps as I recall my conversation with Wendy. I return to the porch where Phyllis sits in the bright sun. "The garage is a mess. There are boxes of our school stuff. What should we do with them?"

"Can you bring them in?" she asks. "I'll look at them."

I haul in one box and go back for the other two. When all the boxes are in, Phyllis decides quickly about box one. "These are the plan books with students' grades," she says, as she awkwardly shoves the box away with her foot. "We can toss them, but wait until we look at other things." She sits in a wicker chair and pushes through the mess of old textbooks and materials, some from teachers who preceded her. She pulls out an overstuffed folder. "Here's a pile of evaluations from my students."

We sit side by side in separate chairs. While Phyllis reads one evaluation, I pick up another. We alternate reading them aloud. Phyllis comments on most of them with a special recollection about almost all of them.

I finally got to read a book I had always wanted to read. "He heard about Hemingway but never had a chance to read anything by him," she comments.

The journalism unit enhanced my writing abilities. "They all had to be published. *The Right Track,* the school newspaper did it."

The drama class brought out the best in everybody. "Some could express themselves better by speaking," she says.

You take time to meet with each student. I comment on this, "They liked to be treated as individuals. That's why I enjoyed counseling."

"I think it worked," she says. "I wonder if anyone cares about this stuff."

"I know Wendy is interested. Maybe we can sort it out, so someone can use it," I suggest.

Exhilarated by the evaluations, Phyllis dives into the third box. Folders, with copies of the materials that she distributed to her classes over the years. Samples of students' work. Photographs. Evaluations from the principal and co-workers. Manila folders stack up around the chairs. The blue plastic boxes stand empty, relieved of their burden. "I don't know where to begin," she shrugs, overwhelmed by the mountains of papers.

I pull one list of suggested novels from a pile of thirty. "One folder at a time. One copy of each thing," I say. In all, there are about a hundred distinct goals, and prescriptions to accomplish each of them. Goals for the program. Goals for Advanced Placement. Goals for learning disabled. Goals for all students. Goals for each part of the program: novel, writing, drama, speech, post-graduation plans. "We'll sort them into an order so teachers can use them," I suggest.

"Do you think anybody cares?" she repeats, knowing that this is going to take energy and time.

"I don't know, but it will be a shame for all of this to hide in the garage forever. It's a bright moment in your career. No one else does it, and no one will unless we save it somehow."

"I put in lot of time and effort," she says, half convinced. "Okay. We'll call the book *Whew...Memories of a Teacher'*."

I like the 'Whew' part!" I want this to happen, and I realize that she does too.

"I had forgotten about this until you brought in these boxes. I wanted to make a book."

"Let's do it!" I say, and we begin the book. "I think people would love to know how you did what you did."

Phyllis picks up a folder, glances at its contents and tosses it into one blue box. "This can be thrown out, and this, and this..." as she points to a variety of folders after a cursory perusal of each. I stop her in the middle of designating further throwaways, "Let's look at these a little more closely. Together we can decide what to save."

The sorted papers tell the story of her teaching method based on the principles: all students can learn; they learn from each other; all should have the same opportunity to learn as much as they can. The order of the papers shows how she dealt with Advanced Placement students sharing the same learning environment with regular students and special needs students. Students worked at their own pace, with interesting and challenging materials.

We find a description of her classroom teaching methods published in the newsletter by the Coalition of Essential Schools in 1995:

Phyllis Palladino's twelfth grade classroom 'has no back,'...no place into which a timid or reluctant learner can disappear...At tables and chairs grouped around the room, students work together on one of four separate unit projects, with the teacher moving quietly from one to another. Several kids gravitate to a raised carpet platform that extends into the classroom as kind of a stage. At one station, a student with reading difficulties can listen with headphones to Sartre's No Exit on tape while others read it in print. On a large "quoteboard" students post memorable or familiar references they come across in movies or outside readings.

"We have to put this in somewhere," I say holding up the newsletter.

"It says it all," she agrees.

In another box, Phyllis finds a wooden whistle. She blows on it, "Wheeoowoo!" reliving the signal that was given over the loudspeaker announcing that the newspaper, *The Right Track* was ready and for sale. In a final tribute to the classroom where every student felt wanted and at home, Phyllis chooses one poem from *The Right Track.*

> *"Metaphor:*
>
> *A poem is like a teacher*
>
> *it instructs*
>
> *it supports*
>
> *it inspires*
>
> *The good ones get under your skin. "*

"Put *written by a struggling student* next to this," she says.

This becomes the final page of the sixty-seven-page book. Phyllis's organization as a teacher makes the book easy to assemble. I labor several hours during one week to format the pages on a word processor. The book represents a lifetime of a cutting-edge teaching. A "how-to" teach and engage students in the process.

"Let's take it to Staples to get it printed," I say pounding the pages on my desk to make them even.

"We can do a few copies," she says.

I want the world to have copies. "We'll do ten."

I think we should present the contents to some teachers' groups while Phyllis still has the ability. As she sleeps, exhausted on the sunny porch, I wonder about that possibility. She tires easily. She gets embarrassed when she makes mistakes while speaking. She expects me to finish her thoughts and sentences. I realize that the time for presentations has passed.

We have reduced the three large plastic boxes to one book. The boxes are emptied. We have ten copies of a groundbreaking teacher's manual. I mail it to a few of the educators that were involved in supporting Phyllis's innovative style. A week later, Wendy stops to visit, clutching the book. "This is terrific. I just came from a meeting. A question came up about the senior program, I pulled out Phyllis' book. Read it to them. End of discussion."

21. Florida

Pat and Maureen O'Brien have been my friends since before Phyllis and I were married. Pat was a Christian Brother and Maureen a Sister of St. Joseph. They both renounced their religious vows and I had the honor of officiating at their wedding. Maureen replaced me as guidance counselor at Vincentian Institute, when I decided that I no longer could be effective in that position and continue to love Phyllis. Maureen and Phyllis became great friends. Pat and Maureen became confidants for Phyllis and me as we made our plans to leave religious careers and get married. Since then, all of us have had successful careers in public education. Upon retirement, Pat and Maureen had moved to Port St. Lucie, Florida. They wooed us with stories of the sunny weather, perfect temperatures, and year-round outdoor activity. When I call them with the news about Phyllis's book, they are anxious to read it.

"Come down here so we can talk about it," Maureen urges us with excitement welling in her voice during a phone call.

After driving three days, signs herald proximity to Savannah. We're feeling tired. Phyllis pulls down the sun visor on the passenger side and checks her face in the mirror. Her hair sits flat, the normal springy curls flattened by the humidity.

"I have to get my hair done. I want to look good when we see the O'Briens," she says.

"Okay. We'll be here a couple of days. We can take care of your hair. I need to relax," I say, realizing that there's laundry to be done. "We need some time off the road."

At the front desk of the Comfort Inn in Savannah, Phyllis asks the manager about a beauty parlor. "There's a group of hairdressers around the corner," he says. "A lot of our guests go there. Never any complaints. They do walk-ins."

"Your hair is our care," the voice says as I call to make an appointment. "Tomorrow at ten is fine, hon. Oh. it's for your wife. Phyllis. Wash and set. No problem."

We arrive at 10 the next morning. "What are we gonna do today, sweetie?" the receptionist asks.

"A wash and set." Phyllis replies.

"How do they do that where you come from?" Phyllis has difficulty with this unexpected question from the receptionist. For the past twenty years, I have accompanied Phyllis to "Tress," where Meryl has set her hair with a curling almost every week. During the past five years, when Phyllis had trouble speaking after the biopsy, I stood close and conversed with Meryl every Friday morning. We discussed politics, or the latest story about pedophile priests, or octo-mom, a woman who gave birth to eight kids at once. We recounted our Italian roots and the old days. We laughed a lot, got angry at crazy things that happened like school shootings, and shared the vicissitudes of daily living with prominent health issues. Time in the hair salon was pleasant for all of us.

Fridays with Meryl became my course in hair styling. I learned how to shampoo and condition; how to apply mousse; the art of curling with a very hot iron and combing out the curls. Lots of hair spray is the finishing touch. I explain the usual half-hour wash and set process to the Savannah hair-dresser. "You just need

126

a little mousse, the size of a walnut, blow dry, and curl it. Comb it out and apply hairspray. It takes about half an hour," I explain pointing to Phyllis's hair.

"Okay," she replies, "take a seat and someone will be right with you."

The double wide trailer beauty parlor has only four chairs. It would be severely cramped if others came to wait during that fifteen minutes. A different hairdresser gets our attention. "Your turn, honey."

Phyllis is ushered to a tilt back chair near the sink for the shampoo. A trickle of warm water and a heavy lather obliterates all trace of the curls. Only Phyllis and I have an image of the style that she wore when she walked into the shop. The cheerful attendant towel dries Phyllis's hair and applies a baseball size dose of mousse. The mousse is left on for a while, and then the hairdresser combs it through Phyllis's hair and dries it. A repeat of the shampoo process, a second generous dose of mousse is dried in. I'm a little wary of the process. I whisper to Phyllis, "I wonder what's next?"

She rolls her eyes, willing to let the process play out. The third trip to the sink, and another application of mousse, concludes with a parade to the styling chair. Progress, I think. This will finally get done.

The curling irons of different sizes rest on a rack over a counter top gas furnace. Electric irons are nowhere in sight. The mousse is slightly dry as the curling begins. Smoke billows from the damp-seared hair fibers. I notice similar pyrotechnics at another station. This is normal. Smoke, chatter, and an endless supply of mousse. The curls are completely sculpted an hour after Phyllis sat in that chair. With the mousse laden curls combed out, and a heavy dose of hairspray, the only part of the process that I recognize as normal, Phyllis stands and admires her new do. "I have a helmet. This will never come out."

A nap, a late afternoon shower, high humidity. All fail to penetrate the helmet. The final day of travel goes quickly. I stop as soon as we turn onto Sandburg Avenue, about two doors away from the O'Briens. I pop open the trunk and rummage to the back of the cargo area. I shake out our winter coats that have been crumpled there since New Jersey. "Let's put these on," I tell Phyllis. She understands my humor. Clad for snow country, I press the doorbell at the O'Brien house. We're sweltering as we wait for the door to open.

"They're not going to believe this," I say to Phyllis through my suppressed laughter. She can't talk because she is also laughing so hard.

Maureen gasps as she opens the door and then howls with laughter. "Wait till I get my camera!" she exclaims. "Pat, Pat! They're here."

Her laughter is uncontrollable. We explode laughing too from deep down in our gut. It's hot! Maureen comes back, snaps our picture, "That's a gem. Come in! It's so good to see you." Pat steps forward in a fit of laughter. After big hugs from Maureen and Pat, we shed our winter coats, hats and gloves. We all laugh practically speechless for five minutes, in shock and surprise. We are together.

At the first break in the gaiety Phyllis quips, "I can't take off my helmet." We laugh some more as we recount the two hours at the Savannah hair salon and tour the house sipping New York State white wine.

Phyllis sports her helmet for the duration of our trip, through the day at the beach, the long walks around the neighborhood during the cool evenings, and the Mets last game of spring training at the ballpark in Port-St.-Lucie. It endures swimming in the O'Brien's pool, hot showers in the morning, and sweaty sun hats in the afternoon. We decide to make a lasagna dinner one night. Simmering sauce and boiling steam of lasagna noodles do not touch the helmet.

Pat proclaims the lasagna a success. "So is your book, Phyllis. Dan would love to try some of these ideas in class," Pat says. Their son Dan teaches at a magnet school in New York City.

"Whatever helps," Phyllis says.

Pat and Maureen O'Brien encourage us to pursue another publication. "I like the 'Memories of a Teacher Book', but you should do something with the stories that you wrote when Dan and Meg were little," Maureen insists.

"I didn't think I would publish them. I just wanted to save the memories and share them with people who knew the kids, especially their grandparents," Phyllis responds.

"Well they are excellent stories and have a universal appeal," Pat suggests as he dips a round of bread into the olive oil plate.

"I don't know if we're up to that," I counter. I slice a crusty brown piece of lasagna with the edge of my knife. "It takes energy."

A day later, it's time to head North. They want us to stay. Only a promise to return soon frees us from their enduring hugs.

That conversation about publishing the stories of Dan and Meg remains fresh on my mind. We discuss it a little on the way home. Of all the articles that Phyllis had written over the years, her creative talks to students, teachers and administrators, only the stories about Dan and Meg originate from motherhood and family life. She presented them in a binder to my parents as an anniversary gift in 1981. Pat and Maureen have urged publication since they first read them back then. I want Phyllis's stories to join the other book out in the world.

"You know, the O'Briens might be right on this. Maybe we should try to publish those stories," I think out loud.

"It's a lot of work; I don't have the energy," she responds.

"You're pretty good now. I know it's a lot of work, but I'm willing to try it," I say. That's as far as the idea gets on our way home. We have too many places to see. Phyllis's helmet remains invincible for another week as we travel through St. Augustine, Charleston, and the cherry blossoms in Washington, D.C.

The snow is melting across the New York State Thruway as we travel past the first tollgate in New York. Snow patches dapple the hillsides as we enter the embrace of the Austerlitz mountains. Snow surrounds our muddy driveway. Snow is

130

evaporating the next day when we visit Meryl, where the remnants of the helmet are removed, and Phyllis's fresh cut and auburn curls are restored. We regain control of life.

There is still at least a month before the Austerlitz springtime, that starts a month and a half after the official calendar spring. With the furnace roaring in the cellar beneath me, I work surreptitiously on *The Adventures of Dan and Meg*. "What are you doing?" Phyllis asks on a sunny morning a week or so before Easter.

"Take a seat and look at this." I move a chair for her next to me at the computer.

The colorful drawing of a bright red fire truck appears on the screen next to the one-page story *The Fire*. This is Phyllis's earliest story. It's one of Dan's first drawings. I, a volunteer fireman, had rushed out to a fire call. The fire truck screams by the house with me riding shotgun. Dan and Meg are excited as they stand at the front window. Then Dan marches around in my snow boots. The story concludes:

"Mama, when I grow up, I want to be a fireman like Daddy," said *Danny.*

"Well Mama," said *Meg, "When I grow up, I might be a nothing, like you."*

"Oh, boy!" said *Mama."*

Phyllis is excited to see the layout, so I show her another story and picture. "I didn't know you could do this!" she exclaims.

"With time, I can do almost anything," I answer. The book takes a shape. In a couple of weeks, I'm confident that it is set up and edited well enough. "We'll go to that printer in Troy to see what he can do with this. It's ready."

The manager at Brown Printing in Troy checks out my CD with the 24-page book on it. He gives us a price, and we pick up a thousand books a few weeks later, five boxes, two hundred per box.

We bring several copies of the book to Tress, the hair salon, and get some positive feedback. Phyllis becomes a celebrity. While Meryl cuts Phyllis's hair, the owner of the Chatham Bookstore offers to have Phyllis do a book signing event at the store. After we set a date, the owner sends out invitations to the event to about fifty of our friends. The friends crowd into the tiny store in downtown Chatham. Phyllis had touched their lives in some way throughout her career. They want to hear her read, get her signature with a few thoughtful words. Phyllis dispenses with the reading. They tell her what to write.

Instead Phyllis says, "I'll just write 'Phyllis'; that's all I can do today."

A Herculean effort enables her to write "Phyllis" about fifty times that day. Phyllis had done this at Autumn in Austerlitz a few weeks before. I realize the limits of the book tour. I distribute some of the books to other local stores without fanfare. Dr. Spinner enthusiastically takes several to put into the children's library at Albany Medical Center. Some become gifts at Christmas, but the supply dwindles endlessly. At the 2005 Blueberry Festival, we set up several tables near the pancake breakfast line with crayons, paper and several copies of *The*

132

Adventures. Parents take time out of line to read the stories to their children. Phyllis signs several books.

"I like your shirts," one parent comments. The cover of *The Adventures of Dan and Meg* is decaled above the shirt pocket.

"These are our kids," Phyllis says as she signs "Phyllis."

***Phyllis signs "the Adventures of Dan and Meg at the
Chatham Bookstore, with owner Muriel Faxon, 2005.***

22. Baked Beans and Pizza

Shortly after the publication of *The Adventures of Dan and Meg*, a little over a year after chemo ended, Dr. Spinner informs us that the tumor seems stable.

"We can stretch the MRIs and visits out to four or even six months," Spinner suggests.

I feel like there is a graduation of sorts happening. The good news brings renewed hope, but comes with Spinner's warning, "It will not always be stable. You are not cured."

I accept this as fresh air, and review quickly future choices for treatment. "If the tumor becomes active, we still can have a chemo re-run, and there is still a possibility of radiation?"

"Yes," Dr. Spinner assures us. "Remember, it's not if. It's when. Meanwhile enjoy your life."

We're euphoric as we leave the office and make a four-and-a-half-month appointment. The secretary and nurses in the area understand our situation. Celebratory hugs come to Phyllis, as if she has conquered her fierce opponent.

In the parking lot, I make phone calls to Dan and Meg.

"What are you going to do now?" Meg asks.

"Enjoy life," I say. "But first we're going to pick up a pizza in Chatham."

"That's a good start," she says.

"We'll go to Williamsburg again soon," I say looking at a smiling Phyllis.

Our spring trip to Williamsburg is easy compared to other years. Phyllis packs her own suitcase with extra warm pajamas in case it gets cold. She uses the map to follow our journey through the less trafficked but still congested eastern part of Maryland. The two-day trip gets long near the end, but we land safely in Patriots' Place, five minutes from the Historic Area. Our apartment is on the first floor.

At a mock trial at the historic town hall about some quirky colonial law, I'm tempted to participate, but Phyllis's firm grasp prevents me. "Let someone else do it," she whispers.

We walk in the sunshine from the town hall to Chowning Tavern for lunch in the outdoor cafeteria.

"They have baked beans on the blackboard. That would be vegetarian," Phyllis observes. "We can get a corn muffin, too."

I order the baked beans and corn muffins for us, a frugal ten dollars. We sit in the sun where a brisk breeze sends a slight chill through us until we open the containers of beans. The homey flavors of molasses and brown sugar whet our appetites.

"I think there are peppers in these beans," Phyllis says. "I'm beginning to feel warm all over, like the hot flash I had once."

We savor the tastes, soft beans, Tabasco, tomatoes.

136

"I love the beans. I wonder if we could get the recipe," she thinks out loud.

We finish our lunch, wash it down with our own bottled water, and wander towards the kitchen area. A woman in colonial dress is cleaning the tables.

"Do you give out recipes for items on the menu?" I ask.

"Some are in the Chowning Tavern cookbook. What recipe did you have in mind?" she says relaxing from her chore.

"Baked beans. Is that in there?" Phyllis asks.

"I don't think so, but I'll get it for you," the worker says, as she disappears into an office area.

After five minutes or so, the worker returns with a printed recipe. "I hope this is what you want. It's for a large quantity."

"Oh, we like to feed crowds," Phyllis says. "We have a lot of relatives."

With a big smile, the worker hands me the paper, "I hope they all come."

"Thank you, we hope so too," I say, and we retreat to a bench near the fire.

"Let's see. Forty portions. Perfect," Phyllis says and continues, "Five gallons of molasses. 12 pounds of brown sugar. 6 gallons of ketchup."

"Whoa! Wait a minute," I say, "How big are the portions?"

"Oh! ah! Portion. One gallon," she laughs.

"That's a thousand servings!" I exclaim, "we can invite the whole town, plus the relatives."

"Well, you can figure it out, so we can have it for a smaller party." She folds the paper and puts it into her handbag. "It'll be delicious!"

The next day we return for lunch but go to Shield's Tavern at the other end of the Historic District. We order the grilled vegetable trencher. *Herb-grilled Vegetables served up on Flatbread with Hummus, Basil Oil, and Tavern Fries.*

"This looks easier than the beans," Phyllis notes.

As we leave the Tavern, music emanates from the street. The Colonial Drum and Bugle Corps warm up for the afternoon parade.

"Let's go, Phyllis. They're waiting for us." We join the crowd on the street. The band marches by. *Yankee Doodle* has everyone clapping and cheering. We attach ourselves to the end of the parade with hundreds of others. *Simple Gifts* slows the pace a bit. More of *Yankee Doodle.* My heart pounds with the drums. The fifes terrify my ears. Phyllis and I wave to the spectators as we sprightly march the four long blocks of Duke of Gloucester Street. It's our parade. We're on the verge of revolution.

138

It's a beautiful day for our return trip home on Sunday. At Newark, Delaware, we decide to rest for the night.

"Let's drive back to the Pizza Hut for dinner. It's not that far and we won't get lost," I suggest.

I smell trouble as I get out of the car. Several kids are running around the lot, playing dodge ball, bouncing the ball off the building. I park at the farthest end of the lot to avoid them.

"What do you think?" I say to Phyllis.

"They're having fun. I'm hungry," she replies.

I assume that what's in the parking lot stays in the parking lot. Wrong! What is in the parking lot is an overflow of activity from inside the Hut, where a little league team celebrates a final game victory for the season. The kids are high from the win, from the pizza and soda. And from the freedom that comes when no responsible adult guides or controls them.

We figure the situation is temporary, take a table, and order a pizza. Our hunger yields to the comfort of that warm round pie oozing with mozzarella. The bedlam around us is an annoyance. The waiters dodge the boys who have been running all over the place. I talk to the manager who shrugs his shoulders, "What can you do?"

Phyllis stands up in the middle of the chaos and shouts "Stop everything!" So much for aphasia. The uncertainty in her speech disappears. I'm aghast at what might happen next.

Her assertive voice causes an immediate calm. Boys stop dead in their tracks. Waitresses stand rigid. Customers are agape with dough filled mouths.

"Who's in charge of these kids?" Phyllis demands in her teacher voice.

No one steps forward. A man with his backward-facing baseball cap hides at a table; a few kids surround him. He avoids Phyllis's blinding glare. She knows this person who may have occupied a seat in her classroom a few years ago and marches straight to him. He stands as she approaches.

"Why do you let these boys run out of control? If they behaved like this on the baseball field, you wouldn't tolerate it," she asserts standing tall to reach his eyes.

He looks away, but mumbles something about "the way kids are today."

She gets into his space. Stands on her toes. Nose to nose. "You're in charge, so measure up. They look to you for leadership! This is a teachable moment, and you blew it."

I pay the bill in the silent moment that follows before the applause as we exit into the parking lot. She's doing okay I think as I help her fasten her seat belt.

23. Newport, Rhode Island

Newport, Rhode Island is a cherished vacation spot for Phyllis and me. The cliff walk along the Narragansett Bay allows us to peer into the backyards of the plush mansions of the Gilded Age, summer cottages of the Vanderbilts, the Astors, and the Morgans.

Almost every year for twelve years from 1999 to 2011 we visit Newport. We only miss Newport in the difficult years of 2001 and 2002.

We stay at resorts in the heart of town, a short walk into neighborhoods replete with blocks and blocks of 18th century houses, stores, and churches. Walks in this area inspire us to carry on our work with the Austerlitz Historical Society, or to paint our own old house one of the colors found on these historic houses. Phyllis observes that the trim, windows, and frames are painted the same color as the rest of the house, rather than off-setting colors, a more popular style. "Let's do that with our house."

"Next time we paint," I say. "Just name the color."

She points to a black house. "That will work." I make a note of it.

One spring, after the graduation at Dr. Spinner's office that extended our office visits out to four and a half months and reduced the frequency of MRIs, we visit six of the mansions within a few days. Plenty of standing, listening, stair climbing. Stamina unbound.

Our wedding anniversary often occurs in Newport. Dan and Meg come to celebrate at some wonderful place when possible. One year, we walk to the Whitehorse Tavern, a few blocks from our resort. The next year, Phyllis and I dine indoors at the Ocean Cliffs restaurant. We decide to eat there outdoors the following year with Meg. Lunch time entertainment comes from the Bay. The manicured lawn swoops toward the shore. Gulls, geese and ducks dive and dine in the blue waters.

Another year, we walk five blocks with Dan and Meg along the waterfront to the heart of downtown to The Red Parrot, a trendy pub that offers sweet potato fries with a molasses dip, and open windows that allow us to gawk at passersby who are gawking at us. The walk back to the resort is broken by a stop at Ben and Jerry's.

The following anniversary, Dan joins us, and we aim again for the Red Parrot.

"I don't think I can make it," Phyllis protests.

About half way, the Gas Lamp Grille beckons with glowing lanterns. Patio doors open to the street. We find a table indoors close to the doors where we enjoy the breeze. The street sounds of car horns, roaring motorcycles and people conversing. Foreign tourists march in a loose column behind a barking guide with an umbrella. Two chocolate Great Danes open pathways through the crowds for their masters. The comfort of lasagna dispels tiredness.

I become reflective. We have already surpassed the five or six years that Dr. Rush estimated eight years previously. This anniversary in June of 2009, our thirty-seventh, is also an unspoken celebration of passage into the ninth year of life with a brain tumor. I don't talk about it. Phyllis doesn't either. Talk is always of the future, tomorrow or next year. An unspoken determination that this condition will not alter our plan to enjoy life, travel and party with friends and family, and be normal.

It's time to paint our house.

"You do like the black on that house we saw?" I ask Phyllis as we walk back to the resort.

"Uh, huh."

"And the red door?" I ask.

She nods yes.

"Do you want me to help paint?" Dan asks, coming back to the conversation after checking out some classic cars from the fifties coming along the street.

"I'll take all the help I can get," I answer. "Your mother will hold the ladder." Phyllis seems to wilt during the walk. While we rest on a bench, lobster boats are pulling into the marina to rest for the night. When we resume the walk, Dan leads the way five steps ahead.

"I-I-I'm can't talk v-v-very w-w-well," Phyllis says with alarm.

"This is different from usual?" I ask feeling a hard squeeze from her hand on mine.

"Y-y-yes," she replies.

It's more than apprehension. Fear. I hold Phyllis tight as we await the elevator to our apartment. As I attempt to allay her fear, my heart pounds, my head hurts, my knees strain to keep us both upright. Utter silence as the elevator ascends. Dan, who had walked ahead of us and did not hear the conversation, joins us in the stillness. He knows something is going on. He doesn't ask any questions. He opens the door for us.

"We see Dr. Spinner next week," I remind Phyllis as we enter the apartment.

"We can meet for lunch after that," Dan suggests as he hugs his Mom and goes to his bedroom.

After Dan leaves the next day, the remainder of our stay in Newport is quiet. I don't ask any more about her speech. I concentrate on assuring that Phyllis has a reasonably good time.

"Let's leave a day early. Rain here today and tomorrow. I can pick up the paint for the house," I tell Phyllis after a quick check of the weather channel.

Deep Charcoal is the blackest house paint that we can find on any of the color charts. I have the dealer mix four gallons to start. It's going to take time to paint this house. It's large and parts of it are high. I know that I need help.

"I'm going to call Lisa to help me paint the house. She needs a job."

Lisa is Meg's childhood friend who has just returned from California. We call her our second daughter. Lisa is happy for the opportunity to help me out. I do the ladder work. Lisa holds the ladder and learns to glaze the windows. She likes puttying. One garage bay becomes our work center where we store the supplies and any windows that are removed for glazing. Lisa works on the windows in the garage during an extended rainy period.

We keep our appointment with Dr. Spinner. In the small waiting room in Dr. Spinner's office I remind Phyllis, "We are going to talk about the speech problem."

"Y-y-yes. Sh-sh-she sh-sh-she should know."

A scratch of fingernails on the door, "May I come in?" It's a time of reckoning instead of the normal good news type of visit.

Phyllis is alert enough to notice that the stool that Spinner usually sits on is missing. She sees one in an unoccupied room across the hall and retrieves it for the doctor. Despite Spinner's insistence that the stool is not needed, Phyllis persists in delivering the stool for the doctor, who appears dismayed by the burst of energy shown by Phyllis.

"You didn't have to do that, but thank you," Spinner says to Phyllis, as she perches herself on the stool. "You seem to be doing very well."

Phyllis smiles, "P-p-problems…"

"Phyllis has been concerned about her speech," I tell Spinner. "She seems to be speaking a lot less. It's an effort."

"How do you feel Mrs. Palladino?" Spinner asks with her eyes concentrated on Phyllis.

"Okay. I-I-I have t-t-trouble. Can't t-t-talk," Phyllis utters apologetically.

"I'm not surprised. The MRI indicates a change. It's time to try something else," Spinner asserts.

"Chemo?" I ask.

"We can try again. It might work," Spinner says.

After eight years of hoping for a cure, hours upon hours of searching online for breakthroughs in the treatment of benign brain tumors, nothing has materialized. A site dedicated to brain tumor research often reported "Results, not as good as we hoped; but it is still too early to tell."

Radiation therapy remains the last arrow in our quiver.

Within a week filled with faint hope, we begin the chemotherapy. Five powerful pills swallowed over the first five days of the cycle.

The house painting provides a distraction from the problem. Phyllis sits near the driveway and supervises for about an hour a day the first week. I stand on a low flat roof, dancing and singing into the paint brush.

"St-st-stop. You'll f-f-fall." She laughs but is fearful.

I keep far away from the edge. If she stands to go to the bathroom, I scramble down the ladder to help her into the house. Frequent falls are another symptom that have become apparent of late.

***

One sunny afternoon, as I cut the grass, Phyllis and Pat sit on the deck under the awning. I doff my straw hat about twenty times as I ride by. They wave. When the lawn is cut, I park the small tractor in the garage and close the overhead door. The car's home is the driveway while the house gets painted.

After I walk Phyllis in from the porch to the den, I prepare tacos. We eat, watch the news, and cool off with mint chocolate chip ice cream. *Dancing with the Stars* mixes live music, gentle repartee with the beauty of dance and a modicum of suspense. We pick our favorite dancers and enjoy the show. Togetherness.

We continue to take comfort in being close. Caressing. Entwining. Oblivious to the world within and without.

The next morning, I help Phyllis shower. I massage her back, arms, legs with jasmine oil. She deserves this and more. After a light breakfast of bagels and creamed cheese, Phyllis relaxes in her chair while I go to the garage to begin a day of painting. Lisa is on her way.

The automatic garage door opener fails, but the dark looking door opens easily by hand. A black film covers the windows, walls and rafters. The stench of burned out fire permeates the air. I barely inhale, hardly able to catch my breath before I have a coughing spasm. White plastic water pipes stored for years in the rafters are melted together with black vinyl sewer pipes, drooping into the work bay. Black and white stalactites. Plastic bottles on shelves bow over, bleeding colored liquids into dark pools on the floor below. The tractor, a melted mass, the victim of its own battery. Apparently, the lack of oxygen in the garage suppressed the fire before it reached the plastic cans of gas and kerosene stored nearby. Soot has crept into every gap: keyholes, electrical receptacles, nail containers. Bicycles, tents, chairs stand tarred in dense grit.

"No work today." I tell Lisa as she pulls into the driveway.

We study the eerie scene. Contorted. Bizarre. Surreal. Like Salvador Dali's melted clocks. Lisa is stunned. We try not to breathe, as we peer at the dead tractor. The paint cans and brushes are covered with black ash.

"Let's go tell Phyllis. What a mess," I comment. Phyllis is in her chair where I had left her.

"We have a problem," I begin. I tell her the ugly story. "I-I-I w-w-want to s-s-s-see."

I help her to her feet. Lisa opens doors as I guide Phyllis to the back door and to the driveway. She coughs as we approach the garage. Lisa stands with her while I open the other door to reveal the burned tractor hulk.

Uniform speechlessness envelopes us as we gaze at the destruction. The stench drives us back into the house.

148

"So, no painting today. I must call the insurance company and figure out what to do. Want a cup of coffee, Lisa?"

"I can't stay," she replies. "I just came to tell you that I got a real job with health benefits. I have some things to do to get ready."

I knew this was coming. "Congratulations!" I say as Lisa hugs us both.

She manages to tear herself away. "I'm a bookkeeper at the nut factory in Chatham. I'll bring you some nuts one of these days."

She's happy. We'll miss her, and we know she will be back.

I call my insurance agent. The claims adjuster arrives almost immediately.

"This looks like $30,000. Everything must be cleaned or thrown out. The bikes are useless. Walls and ceiling need to be covered. Shellac will seal off the odor. It's not just the mower," he proclaims.

House painting becomes garage restoration. The puttied windows get cleaned first, painted and put back on the house. I take a week to empty the garage. Lots of things get tossed into a dumpster. Salvageable stuff gets placed outside and covered.

When the garage is empty, Dan comes nightly for a week. I walk Phyllis to the driveway the first night, so she can take a picture of us decked out in white splash garb, masks, hats and gloves. Soot busters doing battle with a blanket of darkness. Or sterile surgeons dressed to avoid contamination. Throughout the week, Dan and I power wash the interior, and spray everything except the windows with white shellac. The garage glistens. If only life could be this simple. At the end of a week, Phyllis inspects the progress. "W-w-we c-c-can s-s-sleep h-h-here," she suggests with an admiring glance. She surveys the scattered articles on the lawn. "A-a-all the s-s-stuff."

"I don't want to put it all back in. We can clean it and have a tag sale," I suggest.

It's three weeks before Labor Day, a common tag sale weekend. I think Phyllis can work with me with a rag and pail of water. Partners again. The next morning, before I can fill a bucket with water, Phyllis suddenly tumbles on the uneven grass. I help her up. No harm. I set up a clean chair under the canopy from where she can supervise. Most of the work is done in silence. I talk about some of the things, a box of cookie cutters that we used to make Christmas cookies. A metal doll house that was hers as a child, still has some of the old plastic appliances. Her black and white pinto pony that she got when she was four years old, turned mostly black by the fire.

It's an effort for her to talk. But we sing silly songs while we work. *The Titanic, Froggie Went a Courtin'. Old King Cole.* I scrub and hand her objects to dry. She places them in a box next to her chair. Some of the things, especially the doll house and pinto pony, return to the garage. The others get a price tag and are placed on tables on the lawn. Together we admire the sale items.

"W-w-where d-d-did all th-th-this come f-f-from?" she manages to say.

150

"Many Christmases, and other peoples' tag sales," I say.

On Labor Day weekend, people come. Neighbors peer into the shining white garage with a fresh gray floor. "Beautiful!"

Treasure hunters come from all over the county to the trove on our lawn. Cash rolls in at the fire sale.

I place a few leftover items on a small table on the front lawn marked "free." A metal file cabinet, an old metal locker, and some building materials all too difficult to clean are free. Within a day, everything disappears.

In the early Labor Day evening, we float on lawn chairs in a sea of whiteness in the garage. The pinto pony stands ready to rock. A moment. "This is like the drive-in." I say, recalling our first voyage into togetherness almost forty years ago when we taught at Vincentian Institute. Then we had each other in a fleeting moment, and an uncertain future. Perhaps never to be together. "We did it!" I say softly.

Phyllis looks at me. She doesn't speak. Reaches for my hand. We stand in unison, a soft hug, retreat to the den, and then to the bedroom. Together.

24. Decisions

A call from Dr. Spinner a few weeks after Labor Day delivers the dreaded news. "The MRI indicates the Temodar is not working. Phyllis needs radiation."

We knew this day would come. While the tumor was inactive, and Phyllis was clinically pretty good, radiation was off the table. After three months of chemo, the MRI confirms that difficulty speaking, frequent falls and decline in alertness portend change. Change is not good. Perhaps the blast of radiation can reverse the now aggressive tumor. Perhaps radiation can give Phyllis a better life for several more years. I'm determined to resist the tumor's fatality. "I'll talk to Phyllis about it and get back to you."

I hesitate to break the news to Phyllis, but I choke out the words. "Dr. Spinner thinks it's time for radiation."

Phyllis says nothing. It's a long moment. The uncertain untrue final arrow. She nods "Okay" and retreats to the den.

"Dr. Spinner trusts that Dr. Graber can help. Graber has years of experience," I say as I follow her into the bedroom. I don't believe my own words. We have avoided radiation for a reason. It's uncertainty. I rush reluctantly to the kitchen to call Spinner who is a step ahead of me.

"Dr. Graber has time next Tuesday to see Phyllis. She has all the information she needs. She's confident that she can help. I'll see you afterward."

153

On Tuesday, we learn that seven weeks of radiation will stretch from mid-October until early December. Weekends and Thanksgiving Day are holidays to rest from the barrage of rays. At a preliminary session, a technician shapes a plaster mask around Phyllis's head. The mask is matched to a CT scan and marked with a Magic Marker to denote the area to radiate.

A nurse presents a form for me to sign. It states: *The procedure is meant to extend life, not to produce a cure.*

A sledge hammer, the certainty of mortality, hits me. There's no guarantee. There's no comment on quality of life. There's no indication that the symptoms will disappear. I don't want to sign, but I know the alternative is fatal. I scribble my name to disguise it.

To do nothing is giving up. We move forward with the treatments. It doesn't hurt. The attendants are vigilant and caring. One comes to the waiting area and walks Phyllis to the treatment room.

I talk to other patients. Some are there for brain tumors. A young man whose tumor was discovered after he had a seizure while driving. "He didn't know what happened. He wrecked the car," his wife says.

A vigorous older man struts nervously and proclaims, "I have a stage four glioblastoma. It's the worst kind. I'm going to beat it."

I admire his gutsy attitude. He's already survived six months since surgery.

We're all voyagers on a sinking ship. Phyllis has made it almost nine years, and probably still has several more years to live than these men, the difference between a benign tumor and cancer. I take comfort in the misery visited on the other victims. A wicked gratefulness.

I put one piece into a 1000-piece jigsaw puzzle spread on the table for both patients and caregivers to pass the time in the waiting room. And another. As I place a third piece fifteen minutes later, the attendant ushers Phyllis back to the waiting area. She smiles like she has come from a spa. Maybe it's not so bad.

Over the seven weeks, Phyllis regresses, especially in her ability to walk. We walk hand in hand the first couple of weeks. Then she tightens her grip on my hand, clings to my arm. About the fourth week, I'm holding her up as she struggles to avoid the black hole that exerts a deathly pull to the marble floor.

We stop. A readjustment. "Let's try again," I encourage her. We had walked through a corridor that was teeming with doctors and nurses, a change in shifts. There was a lot of help if we needed it. Now we thread our way into a nearly empty corridor. With about fifty feet to go to the elevator, we rest in chairs that are part of a waiting area.

"Do you need help?" a receptionist asks as she leaves an office near the chairs.

"We just have a little further to go to the elevator down to radiation," I explain with hesitant confidence.

"I'll be back with a wheelchair," she says as she walks briskly back into the office.

"We can make it," I insist.

The receptionist's persistence quickly produces a wheelchair, locked in place a few feet from where Phyllis is seated. Phyllis breathes relief when the wheel chair comes. "Wheelchairs are around here for your use. Use 'em," the receptionist urges as she helps Phyllis into the chair.

"Thank you," I shout as the she disappears behind the bathroom door.

The wheelchair becomes part of the daily routine. They are stored in open view just inside the door near the parking lot. On subsequent visits, the valet fetches the chair, and when Phyllis is comfortable, he parks my car. I wheel her the length of the building, a city block, to the treatment.

Over the weeks Phyllis shows more stamina and helps more in transfers to the wheelchair. Two weeks after the final dose of radiation, near the Christmas holidays, I present the doctor and staff with a thank-you platter of homemade Italian cookies like my mother used to bake.

Phyllis receives a certificate of completion that proclaims her a graduate of the rigorous Radiotherapy program. She wobbles independently as she exits the final evaluation. For safety, I wheel her to the car.

"I'm tired," I breathe as we exit the parking lot. "Baking those cookies was going the extra mile. I think we need a break."

156

Phyllis perks up and reaches for my hand. "I don't have the energy to do any Christmas parties this year, not for the family, not for the neighbors," I admit. Phyllis looks at me and nods assent. We are united as we bow to reality. Parties are a lot of work. The fun has gone.

At home in the evening, I call my sister Jean. "I don't blame you," she says. "I've been expecting this. Michael and I have talked about it. The party will be at his house." A week later the day before the party, Phyllis and I deliver the gifts to Mike and Patsy's house. For the first time in almost forty years we are absent.

When I phone the neighbors to cancel that party, they understand and wish us well. Perhaps more to the point, some of them didn't know why we had bothered with the party under the circumstances. "Maybe next year," I tell them.

The 29th or 30th MRI, Phyllis counted over almost ten years, shows only a dark void formerly occupied by the tumor. Some contingent brain cells have also departed, collateral damage. The final arrow has been fired. We have each other and hope left.

25. Complications

The garage fire came, and I didn't know it until I opened the door and peered into the darkness. The fire snuck in during the late afternoon or evening of a warm summer day. The effort to clear the rubble, reclaim the garage to make it useful again, drained my energy. The garage never fully recovered. We discovered damage to the roof rafters a year later.

I'm glad for that frigid January day a few years before the fire, when I tripped over those plastic boxes and decided to do something with their contents. "Memories of a Teacher, whew!" took new life on that day. The book and the memories could have been lost in the summer conflagration but are instead a saved tribute to a time when Phyllis and I worked together professionally.

The symptoms that prompted us to use radiation, the final arrow, return.

In January of 2010, Phyllis begins physical therapy at a clinic in Valatie, seven miles past Chatham. She needs to improve her strength and balance. Three visits to the clinic a week. We exercise at home on other days, especially weekends. She places her hands on my biceps. Face to face, we march through the house; then step up and down on a small platform, our Christmas tree stand, to strengthen her thighs.

"I don't want you to lose strength because of a weekend. You are doing so well," I tell her as she walks and steps with concentrated zeal. It seems to be working.

"Are you okay while I put the step away?" I ask as I gently drop her hand.

She nods consent and stands alone while I remove the stand. Thud! She hits the floor with tremendous force.

I don't call for help, but instead I wrestle with gravity. I turn her, so her body is face up and help her to sit up. I move a very low stool close to her back and I'm able to lift her those six inches. I repeat that with a slightly higher stool, another six inches. Finally, after maybe another stool, I lift her into a chair. We are both exhausted after the effort. We rest a while, and then I help her stand. She manages to walk with my assistance, enough to remove my fear of broken bones.

When we reach the den I ask, "Are you okay?"

"I-I-I'll sit here," she replies sinking into her stuffed chair.

On Monday, with recovery fading, I give up the outside clinic. I call Dr. Spinner to set up home therapy. A tall man named Pieter comes.

"We'll get you walking," he announces. His optimism is contagious. He does some lower leg exercises and then helps Phyllis to her feet. He puts his arms under hers and leads a dance throughout the house. I follow cheering them on. Phyllis moves with him, until she's back in front of her chair. Pieter has her do some squats before he gently helps her sit.

"I'll see you Thursday morning, and we'll do some more," he promises.

160

Phyllis is exhausted but happy.

The next night I ask, "Do you want to walk?"

Phyllis musters her cheer and her confidence. I embrace her and slide my arms under her armpits. She rises, and we dance through the house, the same route as the night before. I reminisced about our first dance together after we were married. We chaperoned a middle school eighth grade Valentine's Day dance. No one was dancing, and we showed them how.

"It's like the Queen of Heart's Dance," I remind her. "Just you and I on the dance floor."

When the dance is over, Phyllis grimaces as she sits. When it comes time to get ready for bed, she can't stand. Exhaustion or something else.

I help her onto a rolling desk chair. "Hang on!"

The chair rolls her to the bathroom, and then to bed. I notice she favors her left side. I assume she's tired.

The next morning, I help her dress and again use the office chair to roll her to the den. I hug her for the transfer into her chair; her lips tighten as the seat meets her buttocks.

When Pieter arrives for physical therapy, he's enthusiastic. He does some ankle stretches with her, "Very good," he says and then cajoles Phyllis as he helps her stand. It's difficult. She winces.

"She's favoring that leg," Pieter observes. "I think you should have it checked in the ER."

"How can you tell?" I ask.

"She's not putting any weight on it. I won't do therapy with this problem. I might make it worse. Let's get her comfortable, and then I'm going to leave so you can call the ambulance," he instructs.

When he leaves, I still don't believe there is a serious problem, but I dial 911 and report to the dispatcher. "It's not an emergency, but a possible hip fracture."

"You just need transportation?" the dispatcher asks.

"Yes, to the emergency room at Columbia Memorial Hospital," I say, certain that there is no fracture.

"How's she doing?" the dispatcher asks as other calls seem to be flooding the emergency center in the background.

"She seems comfortable. No screaming or tears," I report cognizant of the other calls that the dispatcher must handle.

"The ambulance is on the way," she says.

The EMTs efficiently pack Phyllis into the ambulance. I follow in my car. When Phyllis arrives at the ER, she's given morphine to kill her pain.

"Your wife is severely compromised because of the brain tumor and her age. We can put her back together, but her longevity is problematic," the chief nurse in the ER informs me with little delicacy.

"What do you mean?" I say not recognizing mortality's face.

"Statistics indicate that elderly or those with collateral health issues have limited years after a hip fracture. There are exceptions. I just want you to know," the nurse says.

When Phyllis returns after x-rays, she seems conscious and aware, but the x-rays confirms a hip fracture. Within hours, Phyllis undergoes surgery.

Pat, Phyllis's sister, does all night duty at the hospital, serving as Phyllis's voice to call the nurse when needed. I stay the

163

third or fourth night just before her scheduled release day. A snow storm is predicted. I want to be there for her discharge to a rehab facility in Great Barrington, Massachusetts, ten miles from our house.

Recovery is daunting. The rehab staff wants to take care of everything: walking, eating, speech. I wonder about how much can be done, but I'm happy that the trained staff will try. Perhaps Phyllis can come out of this better than she was.

Within a week, Phyllis is standing and moving with assistance, and soon pushes the walker rapidly through the corridors of the facility. The therapist holds her with a belt to prevent a fall. The pace of her movement frightens me. It seems to be an out of control effort to keep up with the wheeled walker, at a speed that would never work in our house of uneven floors and narrow doorways. The therapist tries a walker with tennis balls instead of wheels. It's cumbersome, but it eases my concern.

Every morning when I know therapy is finished, I go to the rehab center. Phyllis's wheelchair is lined up with other patients near the nursing station. One aide can keep an eye on all the patients at once. Phyllis impatiently glances around and exudes excitement when I appear out of the congested shadowy corridor. "I have some real coffee and a donut for you," I say quietly, as I hold up a bag from the Citgo convenience store.

She smiles as I wheel her to the room that she shares with a woman about to go to assisted living. The coffee and soft glazed donuts are our secret pleasure. I found out later that the nursing home only serves decaffeinated beverages to patients.

My visits last all day. I escape when Phyllis takes a nap in mid-afternoon. Coffee at McDonald's, pizza at Four Brothers, or a beer at 20 Railroad St. Each coffee, pizza or beer laden with guilt. Phyllis isn't with me. Despite the assurance of two doctors that the fracture occurred when she sat in the chair that night, I think it was the fall on the previous Saturday. Five feet away from me. A fall I could have prevented.

I return to help her eat dinner. I talk with the speech therapist or social worker. The speech therapist wants to do more.

"I can create a folder with the words or pictures she needs to communicate," she suggests with enthusiasm.

Phyllis rolls her eyes. I agree with the eye roll. It's one more thing, and Phyllis is not willing to learn to use it.

We hold hands in the privacy of her room after dinner, she asks, "How long?"

"Soon," I assure her.

I want Phyllis home as soon as it can be done safely. I have acquired a wheelchair from a church that fits through our doorways. At a meeting with the social worker and therapists, I suggest twenty steps with assistance is all Phyllis needs to do. That's the distance between the bed and the easy chair in the den at our house. Since therapists have already walked much farther with Phyllis for a week, I know the goal has been reached. The social worker sets a release date, a total of three weeks in rehab.

The speech therapist constructs the folder with pictures of common things, phrases and emotions. She reviews the words with Phyllis. The folder will accompany us home to be consigned to a shelf in the closet with the cane the therapist gave Phyllis as she left the hospital in Boston almost nine years before.

When the staff comes to get her ready for bed, I make my exit. "Good night. I'll be here in the morning. Sleep well." A hug, a kiss, a hug, a kiss. Not enough time.

Three weeks after entering rehab, Dan accompanies me to bring Phyllis home. I need his muscles. While we wait for paperwork to be completed, an attendant empties a commode near the next bed. "What's happening?" the attendant asks.

"Phyllis is going home today," I reply.

"No one ever goes home from this wing," he says as he leaves. "Good luck!"

I reflect on the attendant's surprise. One person left the wing yesterday. She had been in hospice. No matter how tired, sore, and battered she is, I'm taking Phyllis home. We have hope. I look over the sheaf of papers that I must sign. Coumadin to prevent blood clots has been added to the list of medications. Physical therapy in the home is prescribed. I sign everything. An attendant, escorting Phyllis in the wheelchair, presses the code in a keypad near the door which opens automatically to freedom. Dan and I slightly lift her into the car. Homeward bound.

26. Therapy and Newport

Pieter arrives in the late afternoon after Phyllis has been home a few days. He's full of energy. I wonder what he eats and drinks to be so alive. He makes Phyllis feel important. The center of his attention. She can do no wrong under his tutelage. He assures her, "We'll get you walking again."

He kneels in front of her chair. "Kick my hand. Again, and again." Counting after each kick until ten. First the right leg. Then the left.

"See if you can march. Stay seated. Lift those legs. Good. Are you feeling okay?" he asks after twenty marching steps.

Phyllis nods, and she rests for a moment or two.

"Let's try standing." He bends at his knees and leans forward allowing Phyllis to grasp his biceps, and as a unit with his support, she stands. And sits. Ten times. "You're a lot stronger than before," he notices. "Relax while I put some information into the computer. Then we'll do some walking."

Pieter again bends over towards her. "Okay. Grab my arms."

They travel through the house through the narrow doorways, up and down the wavy floor, over the uneven boards. Pieter does his thing. I cheer the progress and hope for a complete recovery.

In the summer, Phyllis's right leg swells up. Dr. Spinner orders an ultrasound to detect possible blood clots. After observing about ten years of my caregiving, Spinner has confidence in me.

"You can treat her at home. Inject the medication into the fatty tissue around her navel."

I had done three days of these injections a few years before when there were clots. This time, the treatment is three months of shots followed by Coumadin until the clots are dissolved. It works.

In autumn, I pack up the walker and wheelchair for a trip to Cape Cod. There are plenty of places to walk: around a resort, in small towns, and in the Christmas Tree Shop.

The change of scenery is therapeutic. A modern clean apartment, sandy beaches with boardwalks, waves clapping on the shore, kites aflutter in the stiff breeze. Phyllis enjoys all of it in the wheelchair. We stay on boardwalks to avoid the sand.

I become more adept at helping her make the transfer from wheelchair to car, and vice versa. I realize that the part of her brain that controls ambulation and speech has been damaged first by the tumor and then by the radiation. I'm still hopeful that she can relearn to walk.

When we return home, an occupational therapist consultant suggests a shower without a threshold and a shower chair on wheels. The adaptation needed in the shower is like that needed in my mind. Dan comes one weekend and together we build a new shower area to accommodate a rolling shower chair.

Phyllis and I shop at Home Depot for non-slip tiles for the shower floor. A Home Depot employee pushes the cart with the tiles while I push Phyllis in her wheelchair.

That's our last big purchase while driving our Dodge Caravan. It has worked for a long time. It's easy to get out of, but Phyllis required a slight boost to get in. More recently, she uses a small stool. One day, a clerk at Price Chopper helps to get her into the van.

I need to avoid Phyllis having another injury. My surfing on the web no longer seeks cures, but how to safely manage a struggling, sometimes alert partner. Online I search for a deal on a Honda Accord. It's inexpensive and comfortable with wide doors. Getting in is easier than getting out, but it can be done safely.

Transferring into bed becomes a problem. The mattress is too tall and slippery. Phyllis barely makes it. An accident waiting to happen. Online, I order a two-inch lower foundation and a mattress without the extra foam on top. Phyllis can fall into bed instead of having to hop a couple inches to safety.

Online, I shop for a power lift chair to help Phyllis stand. The chair alleviates some of my effort to help Phyllis get up from the chair. She cannot learn to press the button.

Online, I find an inexpensive hydraulic patient lift, commonly known as a Hoyer. It comes with a mesh sling. If Phyllis falls or I drop her in a transfer, she can be picked up easily with no strain on either of us.

Online, I Google advice for caregivers. Most of it I do already. The big one, "get help," I ignore. I survive ten or more transfers a day, from bed to wheelchair, to toilet, to chair, to a different chair on the porch or even an Adirondack chair in the screen house, and eventually to bed again. A nursing home doesn't enter my mind. Phyllis loves this house. She loves to travel. We are involved in extreme togetherness.

Newport is a barometer of our life during these years. In 2011 we go to Newport despite Phyllis's serious decline in ambulation. I don't know what I expect. The Honda is not as commodious as the Caravan. The condo is not built for handicapped people.

Phyllis needs a shower seat. I pack one that comes apart and allows for other things to be packed under and around it.

Phyllis needs a commode. This folds a little, but not easily. It finds a space of its own in the back seat.

Phyllis needs the wheelchair. It too has its place, folded in the back seat.

Phyllis doesn't need a walker. I pack it anyway. We can work on the walking.

It's a traveling menagerie. Necessities for a seriously handicapped person. A blue handicapped tag to hang from the rear-view mirror makes it all slightly doable.

I pack one suitcase with enough clothes for both of us, and a box of food with cereal, coffee, and spices. We're on vacation far from the home scene that seemed to have so many demands. The demands travel with us, occupying no space in the car. I'm on duty in a different place.

Meg and her dog Zeus join us for the weekend. On Saturday, Panera, a short block away, with its outdoor tables is sunny and comfortable. Phyllis remains in her chair at the table. Zeus sleeps in the shade of the table. Meg and I switch off between shopping in nearby stores and conversation with her Mom. Then all of us parade around the downtown mall and back to our apartment.

The topiary gardens, several miles away, pique our interest on Sunday. It's half an hour ride. We didn't know how muddy the area would be after what seemed to be a light overnight rain. The rain sodden paths mire Phyllis's wheelchair. We walk on the paved areas only. It's a short visit.

After a quick lunch, we return to the apartment. While Phyllis rests, Meg takes Zeus for a walk. She discovers the Cupcake Factory and returns with three lushly frosted edible gems. The colors and crumbs get all over us, nose, cheeks and shirts. Super delicious cupcakes. An early 39th anniversary celebration.

On the days after Meg leaves, I escort Phyllis in the wheelchair along the walkways by the marina. We visit the shops, watch the people, and keep an eye on the luxury yachts and fishing boats that ply the harbor.

Around Wednesday, having a good time overwhelms both of us. I venture out alone one early evening while Phyllis is resting. I head to the cupcake factory. It's closed. I race to the marina where the candy store is open. Chocolate truffles. I buy four, neatly placed in a little box. I present them to Phyllis for another early anniversary treat. No crumbs this time, just chocolate and laughter.

"We've had some great years," I toast with sparkling water, "to more years of fun."

Phyllis nods.

The next morning, with a rain in the forecast, we go home a day early.

Phyllis doesn't improve. Another bout with blood clots becomes complicated when hemorrhaging occurs near the site of the injections. As administrator of the injections, a task about which I have mixed feelings, I am again fraught with guilt. Could I have been more diligent? Could I have known the danger of the bruises near the navel?

Hospitalization is required to drain the fluid from around the belly area, and the insertion of a filter to prevent any clots from reaching her heart or lungs. Rehab follows for a couple of weeks. Rehab this time is difficult. Machines are used to safely move Phyllis from bed to toilet and even to the wheelchair. For the most part, therapy produces little improvement. Rehab wants to keep her in the long-term care part of the facility. I want her home.

While Phyllis is in rehab, I squeeze in time for my own cataract surgery. When asked for my date of birth, I give Phyllis's, and must correct it. Dan and Meg visit often. The three of us take in the Chatham Fair for respite. I convince the staff that Phyllis is well enough for me to care for at home. Dan again helps me do the honors after almost three weeks of rehab.

Around Christmas, another hospitalization occurs. Phyllis is weak and dehydrated. After three days, and a weak recovery, the doctor presents me with a dilemma.

"There's nothing more to be done by the hospital. What do you want to do?" he asks.

In all the years of caregiving, this is the first time that I have to decide. Most of the other decisions were relatively easy. Follow procedure and it will work out. In this case, I see a severely weakened Phyllis, unable to help herself. No rehab this time. No more time in the hospital. Possibly long-term care at a facility.

"What do you want to do?" the doctor repeats.

"Can we get an ambulance to take her home?" I ask.

"That can happen," he says.

"Okay. She'll be home for Christmas," I say.

I'm glad that we can celebrate Christmas together at home. Maybe the season will give us some perspective and strength.

That evening, the rescue squad brings her home.

"Call us if you need help," the driver shouts as he closes the back door. I sit with Phyllis in the den. She rests as I think.

What next?

I'm tired.

When she indicates that she must go to the bathroom, I automatically respond. No more thinking. No more feeling tired. We are back to our routine.

We enjoy a quiet Christmas celebration around the big tree.

27. New Life

After the most recent hospitalization, just prior to Christmas, I know time is running out. Phyllis is totally wheelchair bound when we visit Dr. Spinner in January. Physical therapy seems to be ineffective. Phyllis can stand at a table for almost ten minutes. Walking is lost.

"Mrs. Palladino, the radiation didn't do what we had expected. There are no further treatments. It's time to get help from hospice," Spinner informs us. I've heard good things about hospice. I don't think we need that service yet. It's for people who are dying.

As we sit in the car, Phyllis startles me when she speaks. "I'm going to wear all of my good clothes from now on. The ones I've been saving until I got better." The rest of the drive home is quiet.

Hospice calls me based on Dr. Spinner's referral. The nurse comes to explain hospice. "We do palliative care; comfort for the patient and for the family is our main goal. A nurse will manage the care on a weekly basis. An aide will come daily to help Phyllis wash and get dressed and sit with her. She'll even make the bed."

"What about physical therapy?" I ask, looking at Phyllis who seems to be fading in her chair.

"Therapy will end as soon as hospice begins," the nurse asserts.

I have trouble wrapping my head around this. "The therapy is what makes it possible for her to move around, for me to assist her. We need the therapy."

For the first time in over ten years, I ignore Dr. Spinner's recommendation. While physical therapy is going on, I can be optimistic that Phyllis will take some steps. Walking remains a possibility. I refuse hospice services.

I write to Meg in January:

Today, Pieter came to do PT with Mom. The great thing about him is that he makes Mom feel like no one is more important than she is. He brightens the room with his smile and optimism. He was shocked when he heard that we were looking into hospice based on what he knew when he last saw her. He said with utmost confidence, 'We'll get you walking.'

I'm glad he's part of our team.

By the end of February reality is pounding the door, thundering in my ears. Dr. Spinner advises that standing and muscle tone might be the best that can happen; a little help so that transfers are not too burdensome for me, the caregiver, and as preparation for hospice care.

"You need hospice, Mr. Palladino," Spinner declares emphatically.

My hope wavers. I summon hospice, knowing that the services provided are for the acute terminally ill, a six-month time frame or less until cessation of life. I scoff at this. Six months, impossible. We can recertify every six months.

Meg calls, and I hand the phone to Phyllis while I pick up another line. Meg is excited. "I have just come from the doctor. I'm going to have a baby in September. About the time of your birthday."

"Wow! Fantastic!" I say.

"Gr-gr-great!" Phyllis echoes.

"I'm feeling pretty good," Meg says.

Fresh air. Life. Our first grandchild. Phyllis doesn't want to miss this. Her eyes are bright as she seems to ponder the news from Meg.

New life becomes the focus. Almost daily phone conversation with Meg about the birth journey, is stark contrast to the journey being enacted in our home as the hospice nurse, Marge, ministers to Phyllis. She takes Phyllis's pulse and blood pressure. She makes sure she's comfortable. She questions about my health.

Marge observes our interaction, provides hints for care, helps me to relax. She cares with me, talks with me and Phyllis. Marge is elated about the impending birth, but surprises me with "This often happens, a patient stays long enough to be part of an important event."

I disregard that hypothesis. "We have been through a lot together. I'm going to have a party for our fortieth anniversary in June."

"Gee! That's a lot of work," she cautions.

"Until two years ago, we had a holiday celebration with the neighbors, a sit-down dinner for about 20 people. I know what I'm doing," I say confidently.

"It's different now; you have to do what's comfortable. Take care of yourself," Marge advises.

Agnes, the health care aide, comes virtually every day. She bathes Phyllis. I wait in the wings to help with transfers to and from the shower chair. I teach Agnes how to do Phyllis's hair. The mousse. The curling irons. The style. She's good at hair, her own is well-kept blond. She makes the bed daily, and changes the sheets weekly. After the bathing, Agnes brings Phyllis to the porch, where she exercises Phyllis's legs according to a prescription left by Pieter. Phyllis loves the attention of this dynamic young lady who converses with ease while attending to her patient.

Pat, Phyllis's sister, who lives next door, comes across the grass to visit daily at the end of Agnes's time. Between the two, I get a couple of hours for myself. They are lonely hours, often on a mission to get something for dinner. Always rushed. Short conversations with strangers in the checkout lines and smiling cashiers.

My loneliness is broken by my two chosen chaplains. Hospice regards spirituality as important. I told the nurse that I would have my own chaplain. Al and Tom, the men whom I have designated chaplains, were men who had also traveled to the priesthood and departed. They visit Phyllis. When Agnes or Pat are present, Al, Tom and I go for a walk. We talk, stories from the priesthood, reflections on life and death, and books.

"I just finished a book about the wheelwright trade," I tell them. "Written in the 1920s by the son of one of the last wheelwrights in England."

"That sounds interesting," Al says.

We walk among the trees whose wood was used in the wheel making process. Ash for the circular rim, oak for the spokes, and elm for the hubs. These types of wood form a strong wheel, each lending its own strength and character. The pliable ash. The robust oak. The durable elm that only survives today as dead standing trunks. Bound together with a fired steel tyre, the wheel reveals a perfect relationship, like a strong loving human relationship.

All Things Shining is the book being discussed by our book group. Al has the group meet at his house so I can be there. Dan comes to sit with Phyllis on the nights the group meets.

"What do you like about the book?" Tom asks.

"It encourages us to have an attitude of wonder, to look for the shining, and be thankful," I state. "When we care, we shine."

***

After one of the walks, I return to Phyllis in her chair.

"I had a good walk with the guys. Did you have fun?" I ask as I move toward Phyllis's chair.

She reaches for my hand. "I missed you, but you need to get out."

"We planned the anniversary party," Pat says standing to leave. "I'm getting a wheel of cheese, crackers, and a cake."

"Great. We'll get a couple boxes of wine and soda," I suggest while I rub Phyllis briefly on her shoulders. "We'll get someone to bring some veggies. Who's coming?"

"Our cousins in Ilion and Syracuse," Pat says glancing at Phyllis for a sign of agreement. "You figure out your relatives and the neighbors."

"Okay. We'll have the Sunday before June 12th, our actual anniversary date," I say as I take the blank notepad from Phyllis's lap.

After Pat leaves, I guide Phyllis in the wheelchair up the narrow ramp to the kitchen. Dinner is simple. Salad and penne, aglio e olio, garlic and oil. Phyllis can handle short noodles like penne more easily than spaghetti. We retreat to the den after dinner. I help her stand and pivot into her chair, for probably the tenth time that day. CNN has election coverage around the clock. President Obama is campaigning for his second term. "You can figure out who to vote for," I say while Phyllis arranges herself in the chair.

"Obama!" she says with eyes focused on her hero on the TV screen.

"We'll get absentee ballots this year, so we don't have to go to the polls," I tell her. It's a short evening. Phyllis begins to

180

doze immediately after dinner. My time to relax. I call my sisters who will bring whatever I want for the anniversary. They also spread the word among the other relatives, nieces and nephews.

When Phyllis is alert enough to move, I help her into the wheelchair, then to the bathroom. Back into the wheelchair while I brush her teeth. Then to bed. Four transfers. Little dances that end with a slight tug downward. I spread Jojoba oil on her back and gently massage her upper back and move my hands to her lower back. She sighs with the touch. I do too.

Tears well up in me. I kiss her good night as she curls up on her side.

28.Celebration

I hire The Maids' Cleaning service to give the house a thorough cleaning before the anniversary party. The maids remove a generation of dirt from the cracks between the floorboards. The wood floors glow from the front door to the far end of the porch.

"It smells good," Phyllis comments. "Now I have to see what I can wear." She halts the wheel chair by grabbing the closet door. The clothes that stare at her are old, shabby, and all the wrong size. Some date from her teaching years, fashionable for that time, but not at all correct for the anniversary. The remainder are more recent but purchased for and worn more for utility. Elegance has not been a priority for a long time. The sizes reflect the time when Phyllis had gained weight due to steroids, lost weight due to anorexia, maintained a decent weight while on Weight Watchers. "I don't think these are mine. I need clothes," she says dismayed by the poor selection.

"We'll go to the Lee Outlets," I say pulling the wheelchair back and closing the closet doors.

The Bass outlet is my favorite, close to parking, quality clothing, affordable and always a sale. It is not high fashion, but fashion enough. As anxious as Phyllis is to have fresh clothes, she doesn't really want to shop much. I don't either. Get it done. The mannequins are dressed well. "How about that white top? It looks cool," I suggest as I point up to the mannequin on the top shelf.

I find the top on the rack below and hold it up. Phyllis likes it. I find a light white sweater that will fit over it. She knows

183

there are some silky black pants in that closet at home. Shoes are a problem. A "BOGO" sale, "buy one get one," catches her eye. I pick out two summer styles to try. I kneel on the carpeted floor in front of her wheelchair. Her feet have changed from a size 8. I start with 10, and end there. It's a good fit. "They look good on you," I say looking up at her while on my knees. "We can get two pairs, a tan and a white."

I pick up a pair of black dress shoes for myself. Stylish, but not really me. The square toes extend out like clown shoes. I buy them anyway.

Phyllis holds the bags in her lap as I back out of the door, whirl around toward the car. I toss the bags in the back seat. The move from the wheelchair to the car seat takes more effort than usual. The party prep has promoted the weariness that Marge had warned me about.

Late afternoon has become early evening as I pull into the driveway. A quesadilla is all we need for dinner. I give Phyllis her medications and get her ready for bed. The bed has been made by Agnes earlier in the day with fresh sheets. One nice thing that I didn't do. I give Phyllis a back massage with lavender oil. It makes us both feel good.

I rush to join her among the fresh bed sheets. I ignore her puffy face and splotchy arms. I hug her, kiss her good night, and hold her until she sleeps. I sleep well too.

On anniversary party day, flowers from Price Chopper dress up every room. The massage therapist from hospice gets caught up in the planning and brings flowers. Early in the day, Pat has a magnificent cake delivered by Price Chopper. A young woman who helps deliver the cake recognizes me. "You were my guidance counselor. You helped me a lot."

"I'm happy that life worked out for you," I say, astonished at my ability to remember her from over thirty years ago. Kathy hadn't changed that much, but she was one student among thousands.

Pat places a large wheel of Jarlsberg cheese on a huge board and surrounds it with crackers. I set out the wine boxes. Meg and Lisa Stumph are the hostesses. They set up and make sure people get utensils, plates, and glasses. Dan and Mike Dunham assist guests up the front steps, between the half dozen pots of red geraniums lined up along the path.

Phyllis's cousins arrive from Syracuse and Ilion. Over the past few years, they have stopped often, but never at the same time. We take time for a group photo. My brothers and sisters, nieces and nephews swell the crowd.

The neighbors also come ready to party as we did during the holiday parties. It's not the usual celebration. Phyllis smiles a puffy smile. She's weary early on. Regains her composure when Meg and Lisa takes a break from the kitchen and come into the living room to talk. I stand next to Phyllis's chair for most of the time. I hold her hand, releasing it to shake hands with the guests who patiently wait their turn to wish us well. Some just wander through the house, find the food, and enjoy conversation.

Some people seem to be strangers to her, as she seems to them. I reintroduce them. I'm her eyes and her memory. They banter, uncertain if words are registering. Phyllis feels their presence, their handshakes and their hugs. Their love. "It's good to see you." "Remember when?" "We loved your parties."

Some tell her stories from the old days. She listens earnestly, but often misses the point. The fact that the people take time to come, to labor up the few steps that have become mountains for some of them, reminds me that time marches on for all of us. The spirit remains steadfast despite health challenges.

We drink a toast "*ad multos annos*, to long life, forty more years," share the wine and cheese, cut the cake and put a serving for two into the freezer for next year.
***

The anniversary party celebrated our forty years of marriage, and the five years before our marriage when we met in the corridor of Vincentian Institute. The years in which we bonded in love. When we determined that our life together was more important than the celibate paths chosen in our youth.

I emerge from the party brimming with expectation for our first grandchild. Although I'm discouraged that Phyllis is not improving, she survives the first six months with hospice care and is recertified for another six.

I expend greater energy to assist Phyllis who becomes more unable to help herself. Marge notices my efforts in one transfer. There are ten to twelve transfers each day. My determination to care for Phyllis clouds my own desire to live.

Phyllis's wish. Several years earlier, she said, "No matter what happens to me, you have your life to live. Have fun." Her only elaboration on that, "You're free to interpret that any way you want."

Shortly after recertification, Marge suggests that it might be time to investigate a nursing home. "You can still be a husband and let someone else do the caregiving."

I don't really understand this. It's a new twist on *in sickness and in health, 'til death.* "I think I can keep going," I rejoin.

"If something happens to you, you'll both be in trouble," she observes. Exhausted one evening, after several strenuous transfers and near drops, I can't dismiss the suggestion.

The decision to look is difficult. Nightly, I lay Phyllis down. I whisper, "I love you!" and in her cheerful, firm voice she sometimes replies, "I love YOU!" I cherish the opportunity to give her a massage, back, breasts, arms and legs. I want to be with her.

Phyllis knows that good things are no longer happening for her. She doesn't talk about the impending birth of her grandchild. That is not real yet. I think she knows her time is short. She withdraws more often into herself. Staring, dozing, sleeping. Gazing at the TV. Disinterested. In her own world.

Before we married, we discussed our relationship in the terms of the great Arabic poet, Khalil Gibran, "Let there be spaces in your togetherness." We saw love as impossible. We had chosen lives of celibacy thinking that we were called by God to serve Him or Her in a special divine way. If we were to be friends, if we were to change direction, if we were to truly love each other, we needed space to make that determination. We kept a respectful distance in our relationship. It allowed us to grow stronger as individuals. In the absence of physical love, we studied the art of love. We discussed the confection of love. When we married, we were strong pillars supporting the arch of marriage We understood what we were doing when we walked away from our commitment to religion and became committed to each other. Our love intensified through the years and remains so. "Let there be spaces in your togetherness" becomes the mantra that I repeat over and over to myself in the months since hospice entered our life.

We have come full circle. Phyllis needs her space. I don't want to yield that space.

I feel negligent if I don't inquire about the possibility of a nursing home. The truth is, our situation can change in an instant.

From one nursing home, I get "I don't think we can meet her needs." From another, "Our long-term care beds are full, but we will call you if something opens up."

Perfect answers for me. I did what I had to do. I report my findings to Marge. There's a waiting list. We can wait.

29. Birth

Meg calls late in the day on September 11, 2012. "My water broke, but there are no labor pains. The doctor said to stay home until labor begins."

"So, we shouldn't get excited yet. Do you want us to come to New Haven?" I ask loud enough for Phyllis to hear.

"No. Khaled knows what to do," she assures me. Remember his Mom is a midwife."

"Okay, be safe. We love you," I say as I blow a kiss into the phone. I repeat to Phyllis what I know. "Meg's water broke. But there are no labor pains. She's staying home until labor begins. She's okay."

Phyllis nods and smiles. "Should we go there?" she manages to say.

"We'll see what Meg wants. Khaled is helping her and seems to know what to do."

After a near sleepless night, September 12 dawns with the expectancy of new life. Both ends of life are converging. I remember what Marge said about the coincidence of a big moment, like birth of a grandchild, with the time of passing. My wishful understanding of recertification for hospice care at the end of August was that Phyllis and I could continue our unusual togetherness for at least six months. Six months to welcome our grandchild, and usher Meg into the intricacies of motherhood. We want to be there for the young family.

The next day we are filled with anticipation when the phone rings late in the afternoon. It's Meg.

"It's a boy!" I proclaim to all within hearing distance, all being Phyllis.

She looks at me with a surprised joy, like *Yippee! But how did this happen?* I understand her unasked questions, "How's Meg? How's the baby? How big is he?"

"Congratulations!" I shout into the receiver. "How are you doing?" "Tired." I repeat so Phyllis can hear, "sore, but otherwise okay… great. And how much does he weigh? 6 pounds 4 ounces. 21 inches tall. Yes, he is two weeks early. It all happened quickly. Yes, a very short labor. A good way to have a baby. His name is Khaled Hannibal after his father and the great Tunisian general? We'll be down tomorrow, unless you want us tonight. Okay. Sometime in the morning. Get some rest. We love you. Bye."

I turn to Phyllis, "You heard the plan. We'll be up early. I'll call Dan to go with us. Pat is already there."

Phyllis breathes a sigh of relief. For eight and a half months she has witnessed the development of her grandchild as Meg made near regular weekly visits to us. The O'Shea-Palladino line will continue for another generation. We're anxious to meet and hold our little grandson, and to give Meg a big hug for a job well done.

Dan's at the door at about 9 a.m. Phyllis is dressed and sitting in her chair ready to roll. I have a backpack of supplies and goodies. Ativan is in my pocket just in case. "Hi Dan. You got here early." He steps out of his truck.

"Got to see the new kid," and he brushes past me to go to the bathroom. While he's in the house, I help Phyllis into the car. "Ready to go?" he says. "Want me to drive?"

"I know the way," I tell him as I move to the driver's door. "I'll drive for a while."

Phyllis sits calmly in her seat. I take a shortcut through the hills of Sheffield, Massachusetts, and onto Route 8, the main highway to New Haven, Connecticut. When we pass a camping area, Dan recalls a camping trip with Andrew Schnabel on the way to an antique car show in Carlisle, Pennsylvania. Andrew became a family member when he bonded with Dan while working on cars. He lived near us during his middle and high school years. He had borrowed Meg's tent for the trip to Carlisle.

"He did what?" I need Dan to repeat over the road noise.

"Cut a hole in Meg's tent. He had to go in the middle of the night but couldn't find the tent zipper. He slashed an opening; then realized his feet were sticking out the door. When it started to rain, he slept in the car. Plenty of room in the Chrysler."

Phyllis's eyes flash with glee as the colorful antics of Dan and Andrew stream into her mind. I surmise her thoughts. *It could only happen with those two. Where did they come from? My brother Francis was into cars too. It's in Dan's blood.*

191

Within the New Haven city limits, the GPS guides us quickly to the Yale-New Haven Children's Hospital. A valet assists with the wheelchair. "Where to next?" I ask. The valet motions toward the security desk, where we're tagged with badges and pointed to the elevators. We roll up to the elevator. Sixth floor room. There's Meg, holding her precious sleeping newborn.

"Hi!" "Hi!" "Hi!" Meg hands the little bundle to me. "Here's your grandson. Khaled Hannibal. Don't drop him." She rolls out of her bed to hug Phyllis and Dan. Pat comes in behind us.

"He's so little; you and Dan both weighed over 8 pounds when you were born," I whisper.

"But, he's two weeks early!" she exclaims. "I'm just glad he waited a day and wasn't born on 9/11."

Phyllis's eyes display eagerness to hold her grandson. Meg removes the tiny bundle and places the blue blanketed baby boy in her lap. "Here's the next generation." Phyllis delights in the baby lying safely in her lap. Uncertain about what to do next. Afraid to try to cradle him in her arms. Perplexed as if to say, *Is this really happening?* Meg snaps photographs. I do the same.

Precious moments. Life waxing. Life waning.

Uncle Dan has his chance to hold his nephew. Pat glows "O'Shea" when her turn comes. While Dan, Pat and I go for lunch, Phyllis snacks and rests with Meg and the baby. After lunch, we say goodbye. Hugs and kisses all around. We each give the baby a pat on his blue hat. "We'll see you soon, Meg. Love you!" I whisper as we leave the mother and child to nurse.

The trip home is uneventful. Dan drives. Phyllis sleeps all the way. In the late afternoon, Dan helps wheel her into the house and heads back to Albany. Phyllis sleeps for two more hours. When she awakes. I offer her a half sandwich and some ice cream. Phyllis cannot handle utensils, and a sandwich lingers on the plate as if in a glass case, impossible to reach. I place the edge of the sandwich up to her mouth. I spoon feed the ice cream. I move a glass of water to her lips. Small sips. Swallowing is a chore. Togetherness at a meal reflects the commitment of love.

I put her back to bed, and she snores into the night. I have my own sandwich and a glass of wine after Phyllis is asleep.

In the morning, while we rest a little longer, I remark, "What a beautiful baby! Phyllis stares at me as if she had a dream.

Later in the day, we talk about the trip. Phyllis stares at the picture on my phone, a strange photo of a puffy faced, not well, grandma smiling at a newborn grandson. Joy. I don't think she recognizes herself. The baby is her focus. So happy to see the day.

Phyllis sleeps most of the time for the next five days. I know something is happening. Serious bleeding appears in her stool as I put her to bed one night. It continues the next morning as she is bathed.

When Nurse Marge arrives, she examines Phyllis. She motions to me to go with her to another room. "The medications cause this," she says. "We have to remove the drugs to stop the bleeding. Phyllis can't drink enough fluids to recover from this."

"What can be done?" I ask.

"Her system is breaking down, she can't swallow. Hydration in the hospital is possible, but not recommended," Nurse Marge says. Intravenous hydration had been done just prior to Christmas. It was a difficult recovery. Phyllis's body was in better shape at that time. Then there was no hemorrhaging. She could still take in food and drink. She was alert. This time is different. I must let go. The wisdom of Khalil Gibran coaches me. *Let there be spaces in your togetherness. Let the winds of heaven dance between you.* I swallow and hold back a flood of tears. "No hydration. She's staying home. What's the time frame?" I ask.

"It could be a few days or a couple of weeks," Nurse Marge says as she returns to Phyllis's bedside.

I call Dan, Meg and Pat to let them know what's happening. I try to help them understand my decision-making. "It's just too much to recover from."

About ten days after the birth, Meg drives to Austerlitz to see her Mom. The baby is snug in his car seat, a plastic container designed for safety in the car, and in the home. My sisters and Meg's cousin Michelle are also visiting. Meg confesses that she knows little about child care. "I'm afraid to give him a bath. I don't know how to do it."

"We'll show you," my sister Mary offers.

Immediately the class begins. The elements of bathing. Meg produces a small plastic tub. Jean fills it with about two inches of water. On the dining room table, Khaled is disrobed. Jean gently places him in the water, while supporting his head with her right hand, and then proceeds to sponge him softly with the lightly soaped washcloth. Mary pats him dry and hands the fresh smelling baby back to his mother who caresses him and dresses him in his "Onesie." Phyllis watches, unable to participate. Perhaps she realizes that it should be herself who is giving the class. That's what mothers do for their children and grandchildren.

Everyone holds Khaled who stares quietly wide-eyed at his extended family.

Dan, the proud uncle, comes later in the day. He visits his aunts and cousin. When they leave, he and Meg huddle close to their Mom. They know time with her is short. They need each other and time to process the fact that they will soon be motherless. I end up baby-sitting Phyllis and Khaled while Meg and Dan have coffee together at a nearby diner. When they return both Phyllis and Khaled are asleep, while I enjoy the silence.

As she wraps Khaled tightly in his sleeper, Meg promises, "I'll be back soon. There's a birthday party next Saturday, right?"

"Yes. It will be a joint celebration," I say as I pick up the car seat and move toward the door. Meg lingers a moment with her Mom.

September 13, 2012: Phyllis cradles her grandson Khaled Hannibal at Yale University Hospital, while I beam with pride.

30. Birthdays

We had usually celebrated Phyllis's birthday on the 27th of September, and Dan's two days later the 29th. Since the 27th is in the middle of the week, we plan both for the 29th.

The drug holiday, as Marge calls it, has mixed blessings. Phyllis was dazed all those years, the side effect of some of the drugs. Those drugs prevented seizures, reduced inflammation, and improved concentration. The drugs that rendered a decent quality of life have become the enemy. Removing the drugs enhances her awareness. She laughs more.

"I feel better," she says. "Maybe I will blow out the candles."

Morphine kills whatever pain she has, but she's conscious enough to enjoy the fall days that lead up to the birthday celebrations.

Dan comes early to the party. He has trouble doing nothing. He digs out the *Sorry* board game. Phyllis is excited in her chair at the table as Dan and I take turns rolling the dice. Dan rolls for her. Her yellow tokens move around the board faster than his blue pawns or my red ones. She loves it. As Meg barges in with Khaled, Phyllis is declared the winner. It's party time on the vast sunny porch.

Meg places Khaled in Phyllis's lap. "An O'Shea," Phyllis says as she plays with his tiny fingers. She admires his eyelashes. She inhales his babyness.

Meg nurses Khaled through the twice sung birthday song. Dan and Phyllis cut the cake provided by Pat. As the autumn afternoon turns to dusk, Meg and Khaled give a round of hugs to everyone. "I'll call when I get there. Love you, Mom," she says with an extra hug.

Dan also wraps Phyllis with a big hug. "Happy birthday Mom, I love you."

"Happy birthday to YOU!" Phyllis rejoins.

The party is over. I thank Pat for the cake. "Phyllis is tired, so we'll turn in. I'll call you in the morning."

The birthday celebrated 75 years for Phyllis. I could not have guessed that this would happen eleven years ago. "You were very good today," I tell Phyllis. "I have one question, what's your name?"

"Phyllis Jane."

"Thank you!" I hugged her. For several years, I had been giving her name. She knows who she is.

Tired, but not ready to sleep, we watch the last half of a Notre Dame football game. Phyllis likes to see her Uncle Bart's team play. Sometimes he helps them win from his seat in the high heavens, and this night he's very active.

After the Notre Dame victory, I bring Phyllis to the front window. A brilliant harvest moon illuminates the road and the trees on the other side. It's like daylight. She looks out and seems to enjoy it. Normally, she would have kept a fixed gaze or not looked at all. As I pull the cover over Phyllis in bed, she says "I'm glad we had this time together."

"Me too. We enjoyed it. Thank you," lost, as I muffle my tears in her welcoming bosom.

I don't hear much from Phyllis the next two days. Sleep has conquered her. Marge comes and declares that Phyllis is comfortable. Agnes comes and washes Phyllis in bed. Agnes realizes that the sheets are wet and need to be changed. Together, Agnes and I change the sheets while Phyllis continues to sleep.

On Wednesday, my sister Mary and her husband Roger come to visit. They tell me to take a walk. I visit with them for a few minutes until Agnes comes. I report Phyllis's lack of activity, constant sleep, little nourishment, or water.

I walk, and I think for an hour. No signs of a possible rebound. Only decline. I love her. I don't want her to suffer anymore. The commitment of love means knowing when to let go.

There's merriment when I return. Agnes, Mary and Roger announce a miracle. While Agnes was bathing Phyllis, she suddenly woke up. Phyllis talked and joked with them. I'm elated. Phyllis has enough energy for a few more smiles when I see her, but not much talk. A missed opportunity.

Phyllis settles back into sleep. The next few days I stay very close hoping for another burst of energy.

I think positive thoughts. Maybe, escape to the Cape soon. A good way to comeback, reset, bond. Hit the Christmas

Tree Shop. Do some wind surfing. Hike the trails with the baby on our backs. Taste the sand. Ride a dune buggy. Fly a kite(yeah!). Just be people. I dare to dream. Nothing happens except the dour prediction from Marge. "Something is going to happen this week end."

I'm to expect a drastic change in Phyllis's condition. Already, I have witnessed the loss of consciousness, swollen hands, ankles and legs. She is feverish.

This weekend is the 16th annual Autumn in Austerlitz, a festival that Phyllis started and inspired. Every year, Phyllis and I made carrot soup for the Soup Kitchen at the festival. This year, I do not make soup. In the last ten years, despite her tumor, Phyllis has been responsible for initiating the children's parade at the event. Flags, a drum, and an old American song. We enjoyed what we had. No space for Autumn in Austerlitz this year.

Instead, I load up oral syringes, with a night and day supply of morphine and Ativan, and administer it on a schedule. I bathe her on the weekend. I turn her every couple of hours. I keep her mouth somewhat moist with the little sponges on a stick.

The weekend passes without any change that I can observe.

On Monday, I decide that Phyllis needs the whole bed. I set up a twin bed in a corner of the room where I am not more than six feet from her. I don't sleep well.

On Tuesday night, I line up enough morphine and Ativan syringes to last until mid-morning. I do not want to measure dosages in the dimness of a 4-watt night light. It becomes a

200

difficult night again. Her breathing is a hacking snore. At 1:30 a.m., I turn her hoping for more normal breathing. Phyllis is easing out of this life. Her breaths are numbered 9-10 per minute, 600 per hour, about 14,400 by this time tomorrow.

Maybe she needs permission to go to the ultimate space in our togetherness. Permission. Extreme Unction. Last Anointing. Sacrament for the dying. For the final journey.

I pour some lavender oil onto a cotton ball. I begin to anoint her forehead, eyes, ears, nose mouth, hands and feet. The words of the traditional anointing that I had used many years before as a priest begin to surface. Those words that refer to forgiveness of sins committed by the various senses are not the ones I want. Phyllis has no sin.

Strength and blessing to complete her time here are her immediate need. As I applied the fragrant oil to the various parts of her near lifeless body, I used my own words. "May this anointing help you on your way, and give you the mind, the vision, the sounds, the speech, the sense of touch, the strength in your legs, to bring you to your final home." I adjust her pillow again. She breathes quietly. I fall asleep.

I repeat the anointing at 7 a.m. silently. No words.

By 10 a.m., Phyllis has stopped breathing. The fragrance of lavender lingers. Bright sunshine fills the room. I lie next to her. I capture her warmth for the days and years ahead. For Dan, Meg, Khaled, Pat. For anyone who somehow will share in it.

Acknowledgments

The production of this memoir, from when I wrote the first stories, spanned six years. I am grateful to many people who worked with me. Al Stumph has been there from the beginning. He encouraged me to join the Library Memoir Writing Group in Chatham, New York, where I first began to write and share with a small audience. Al helped me to write with a purpose and focus. He made many editing suggestions in the final stages that helped render a succinct, readable work. Al read and heard each individual story many times, and waded through several final drafts, and one proof, each time with diligent attention and insight.

I delighted in reading some stories to the reading group mentioned in the text. After one such reading, Marge McCoy suggested that I write a story about my first Christmas with Phyllis. The visit to Ilion was born. Bridget Beckman, a writer, instructor and friend read some of the stories with me. We both cried through the reading. I was raw from the eleven-year ordeal. She suggested I learn to write dialogue. I didn't know how. I was fortunate to attend a writing group at the Tivoli Free Library where Tommy Zurhellen, a novelist and writing professor at Marist College, answered my question, "How do you do it?" "Start with 'Hello', and go from there," he said. I reported back to him, "It works." Michaela Morrisette, managing editor for *Conjunction*s, the literary journal of Bard College, succeeded Zurhellen as leader of the writing group. She introduced me to some creative and descriptive techniques that make a story more interesting.

My daughter Meg, who is Director of Summer Sessions at Yale University, encouraged me to attend the Yale Writers' Conference in New Haven, Connecticut. There, Jonathan Levi introduced to me the notion of beginning a memoir with a critical incident. I worked at it. He liked my story, and encouraged me to attend the Under the Volcano International Writing Program (UTV) in Tepoztlan, Mexico. He was on the faculty, and assured me that Alison Wearing would offer an excellent memoir writing experience. Wearing worked to get her students to pause in a narrative, to linger a bit on a scene, a person, or an emotion. "Shine a light on it," she suggested. The story of the first Christmas developed further with nuances that made it more human. At a retreat two years later, Wearing led the participants in a discussion of the first chapter, *Myrtle Beach*, which became my critical incident. In the intervening year at UTV, Allen Kurzweil discussed many aspects of memoir writing. "It's a way of holding on and letting go at the same time." How true!

Patricia Fecher, former director of admissions at Columbia-Green Community College, whom I had met professionally when I was a guidance counselor, read and commented on a very long version. I was able to let go of some stories based on her suggestions. Jayne Benjulian, a talented poet and teacher in Great Barrington, Massachusetts helped me to broaden my perspective and to appeal to a wider audience.

In the summers of 2016 and 2018, I had the pleasure of attending a workshop at the Millay Colony for the Arts up the hill from my house in Austerlitz. Colleen Kinder, a gifted non-fiction writer who also teaches at the Yale Writers' Conference, read chapter 20. She perceived it as a wonderful act of love, and asked how much more I had to write. I told her that all the stories for the memoir were written. Kinder asked me how long it would take to get it ready for the printer. When I said ten days, she urged me to get it done. Almost a year from that day, I sent it to the printer. I was holding on and not letting go.

Encouragement came from Mary Scanlan an author and member of the reading group mentioned previously. While recovering from a serious auto crash, Mary read a lengthier version of the memoir which had a different title. She wrote comments, and offered advice on publishing.

My son, Dan, and daughter, Meg, have encouraged me in many ways. I often sent them stories to review. Sometimes they responded with "Great story pop," or "Why don't you leave that part out?"

While visiting San Miguel de Allende, Mexico in February of 2018, I met Beverly Ruth Bader, a psychologist and former English teacher from Hastings-on-Hudson, New York. From an early evening conversation in a quiet cafe, a relationship was born. We easily identified with each other because we had both recently lost wonderful spouses. The mere two-hour drive from Austerlitz to Hastings-on-Hudson enabled our conversation to continue when we returned home. Beverly sat with me for many hours in August of 2018, editing the manuscript before I sent it to the printer. When it came time to design a cover, Beverly's eye for symmetry and color guided the design. When the final proof arrived in June of 2019, we once again sat down to read aloud the entire memoir. My eyes watered. Beverly cried. It was difficult and heart-wrenching. With this publication I am finally able to let go.

Phil